TALES from the SMOKEHOUSE

TALES from the SMOKEHOUSE

Herbert T. Schwarz

Illustrated by Daphne Odjig

Hurtig Publishers
Edmonton

Hurtig Publishers
10560 105 Street
Edmonton, Alberta

ISBN 0-88830-122-7

Printed and bound
in Canada

Contents

Acknowledgments

To Norval Morrisseau and Kahn-tineta Horn
To Daphne Odjig Beavon and Whispering Dawn
To Paisk the storyteller
And to the silent brown men
Who welcomed me into their cabins
As a man amongst men.
To my unknown heroes
Somewhere in Canada—
The simple Indian woodsman
The gentle Indian girl
And to the one named Rosana.
To Grandpa Big Horn
Who gave birth to a calf
And to the white boss who preferred
His dusky Indian maiden to white.
Their stories were told in the sweat lodge
Amidst the hissing and sizzling of steam
As it spiralled towards the ceiling
In search of an Indian dream.

Also to my dear friend, the late Dr. Marius Barbeau, who taught me affection for and appreciation of our native people; to Mr. and Mrs. J. Moran for their invaluable advice; and to Gary Shables who patiently typed my manuscript in the high Arctic, in the middle of nowhere.

Introduction

 *T*ales *from the Smokehouse* is based on personal experiences with Indians in various parts of Canada and is not meant to be a scholarly book. The Indian sweat lodge is seldom large enough to accommodate so many people. In this book I have used it as a stage, and since my storytellers were urgently clamouring for attention, I invoked the Indian law of hospitality and let them in.

The legendary erotic stories narrated in this book do not relate to one Indian tribe in particular. Most of them are Ojibwa; some, like "The Bear Walker," are Mohawk, and "Big One and the Bad Medicine Woman" is Naskapi, from eastern Canada. In spite of this tribal diversity, there is a logical progression of events which reaches its climax in "The Magic Gun." Whenever possible I have retained the Indian manner of expression and thought, with the exception of erotic passages which were impossible to present in their original form, and which I have interpreted in a manner strictly my own. Like all peoples, the Indians have stories of incest, bestiality, polygamy, and castration. These were not told for their own sake; a moral or social truth was drawn from them, which instructed people in the disastrous consequences of social misbehaviour. Thus even the mighty chieftain Nanabajou becomes the subject of ridicule and meets his punishment as he lusts for his daughter. The "he-bear" is killed after seducing a lone woman, and the woman herself, who participated in the act and repeated it of her own free will, becomes a ghost-like creature, half animal and half human. The medicine woman who exploited sex for evil has her head smashed, and the evil Indian who abducted young girls becomes prematurely old.

With the advent of the white man the stage is set for more dramatic events. Confronted with an entirely alien society, little makes sense to the Indian. The old established social mores, freedom and personal dignity disappear, and the horror of "The Magic Gun" sets in. The stories that follow "The Magic Gun" describe the conflict of the old Indian values with those of the dominant white culture.

Some are factual stories. They happened not too long ago, and several of the characters are alive to this day; at times I myself, a startled spectator, was thrown into the mêlée of events.

The "white man's town" of the book does not exist; it is a composite of several places where the Indians and whites live in close proximity.

But enough said—the sun is already setting, a group of Indians leaves the village. Let us follow them.

H.T.S.

To Miromesnil

The
Sweat
Lodge

It was already twilight in the forest when a group of Indians emerged from a deep ravine and followed, in single file, a narrow pathway towards the summit of the hill. Silence enveloped them in the thick forest and the only sound was that of a babbling brook as it splashed noisily over the cold mossy stones in the ravine below.

A mongrel dog from the village followed them for a while but the Indians shooed him away. The dog stood still in his tracks and watched them disappear into the bush. After a few mournful howls he turned and trotted away.

Steadily the Indians ascended the narrow pathway to the top. Some of the younger ones carried packs on their shoulders. The old men supported themselves on heavy sticks and from time to time had to rest until they gathered their breath. Then, laboriously, they continued after the others. Eventually they reached the crest of the hill where the path widened out to a grassy field. A stream ran across the field, twisting and turning until it disappeared among the rocks and cascaded down the steep ravine to the brook below.

The Indians crossed the field until they reached the forest's edge. Here they stopped. The old men sat down on rocks and fallen tree trunks, resting their gnarled hands on their heavy sticks. They sat immobile, their eyes half closed, and gazed into space.

The younger men got busy. They collected rocks and placed them in a high circular pile which they surrounded with firewood. They then lit a large fire. When the stones were red-hot and the fire burning low, they spread a thick pile of cedar branches on the grass around the fire. They built a spacious circular frame over the heated stones with birch and cedar saplings and covered it with hides and blankets. Then they ran to the stream and filled wooden buckets with water.

The sweat lodge was complete and, as an owl let out its ghostly cry, the young men gave a sign to their elders. The silent figures roused themselves and proceeded slowly to the lodge, aided by their heavy sticks. As they entered they discarded all their clothing and seated themselves in a circle around the hot stones. The younger men followed with buckets of water and closed the entrance with a skin.

Outside, the lodge was silent, bathed in the silvery moonlight. Inside the water hissed on the hot stones. Wrapped in clouds of steam the Indians offered themselves to the great spirit of the lodge. They tapped the perspiring stones with sticks and chanted sacred songs to purify their souls and give power to their bodies.

When the moon was high in the sky the ceremonies were completed, and the Indians fell to story-telling.

Nothing could be heard in the silent field, nothing but the eerie hoot of an owl somewhere in the forest.

Blue Sky
Takes a Wife

May the spirit of this sweat lodge uplift my miserable existence. Yes, my Grandfather, I am truly old and there is no one to console me in my loneliness.

"You, Great Spirit, who is so far away yet so near, who has been with us always from the beginning of time, take pity on me, a relic of the days gone by. Yes, Great Spirit, listen to me and let the past be. Bring back the sweet days of my youth and with them the memory of Powomis!"

The men in the sweat lodge listened to old Blue Sky's invocation with respect. He was so old that it was said he knew things long since forgotten, and even that he possessed unnatural powers which he had learned from the medicine men of old.

Blue Sky poured some water over his hot and perspiring body. He looked around at the assembled men and continued: "My brothers, I see questions on your faces. Powomis? We don't know her. Where is she from? Who is she? Very well, I will tell you all you wish to know. Listen to my story."

Many, many years ago, when I was young and full of spirit, a girl called Powomis lived in my village. She was very beautiful and all the young braves wanted her for themselves, but no one craved her more than I.

According to our custom, Powomis, who had reached marriageable age, was put in the charge of two old women. They instructed her in the ways of womanhood. They also guarded her night and day. Every evening when Powomis went to bathe in the river, I secretly followed her. But the two old women were always with her. The more I saw of her beauty the stronger was my passion to possess her.

In the month when everything turns green, Powomis returned to her father's lodge. Now she was free to marry the man of her choice. All the men

15

bigger and bigger until the bag was not large enough to hold it! Suddenly the penis jumped out of its bag and flew straight as an arrow over the creek and through the bush. It whizzed over a bunch of dogs and frightened them out of their wits, scattering them in all directions.

Soon the penis approached the settlement and reached Powomis's lodge. It made a hole in the skin flap and flew straight to the naked girl, burying itself deep in her private parts. There the mighty penis, finding its resting place very enjoyable, at once worked itself into a frenzy. It started to move up and down and thrust deeper and deeper until nothing of it could be seen from outside. Powomis, her private parts so suddenly disturbed, shrieked with surprise and woke everyone in the lodge. The old woman looked at Powomis, who was flushed and sweating. Yet there was nothing to account for her strange behaviour, and she certainly did not seem to be in pain. The old woman, concluding that Powomis was having a bad dream, turned over and went back to sleep. Meanwhile, the mighty penis did not slacken its efforts; it worked up and down and soon enough Powomis experienced a most pleasurable sensation. She shook and gasped, pressing her legs tightly together. Suddenly her body tensed, and then she went limp all over and collapsed in a dead faint. At dawn the mighty penis, now quite small, slid out of Powomis's comfortable hole. Very slowly, it flew back to the leather pouch around my neck. I secured the bag tightly and then, quite spent myself, I went to sleep.

The next night I again undid the strings of the pouch and dropped Powomis's hair into it. The powerful magic worked as before. My penis became the mighty one, flew straight to Powomis and once more the gasping, shaking girl awakened the occupants of the lodge. The old woman was deeply puzzled by her strange behaviour but, not finding anything out of place, returned to sleep. On the third night, Powomis did not go to sleep. Eagerly she awaited the mysterious stranger who gave her so much pleasure. Her expectations were not in vain. Once more the mighty penis lodged deep inside her and commenced his frantic activity. As soon as she felt him, Powomis started calling him all kinds of sweet names, embracing him tightly with her legs, and, soon enough, very excited, she was trembling and shaking and crying. With all that noise, the others in the lodge again woke up. They watched, perplexed but not knowing what to do. Powomis, flushed and agitated, twisted frantically on her fur robes, crying endearments to no one in particular. Suddenly the girl's body became tense, and, after giving a big sigh, she fell fast asleep. The girl must be sick, they concluded, and in the morning Powomis was dosed with medicinal herbs.

They were much relieved when on the following night no noise disturbed their sleep. Powomis rested quietly on her skins, but she was not asleep. All night she waited eagerly for the mighty one to visit her. She called him sweet names, but it was no use. As the medicine man had instructed me, I kept him securely tied in my pouch.

In the morning I visited the medicine man. Again he chanted his magic songs, danced around me and beat on his little drum. He extracted my penis from the bag and deftly attached it to my body. He rubbed my private parts with bear grease and the sacred onaman sand, a powerful love medicine. I paid him well for his services and departed.

I waited several sleeps until the moon was full. When it was high in the sky, I returned to Powomis's lodge. I undressed and pretended to go to sleep. But Powomis was not asleep. With great impatience she waited for the mysterious stranger. When she saw me undressed and apparently asleep she leaned over the old woman and looked me over. Gently with one hand she touched my private parts. My penis, far from being asleep, shot to the sky and became the mighty one. Powomis would not let go of her prize. After some urgent whispered consultation with the old lady she moved over to my side, called me sweet names and continued her caresses. I could pretend sleep no longer. I turned over and made her one with me.

That is how Powomis became mine. We lived happily together for many years. Now I am old. Soon I will leave you all, and like the steam from these sacred stones, my spirit will soar upwards into the great unknown, and there I'll find Powomis waiting for me.

Nanabajou
and
His Daughter

Blue Sky, like you I am a man of the past. But times have changed. There are now two ways, the old and the new. Could we still live according to our customs of long ago? No, that's no longer possible! We are no more as one with the land. Those days are gone and will never return. But protected by the spirit of the sacred lodge, we still have our stories to tell, stories of our people and of days long ago."

With these words, Brown Eagle, a respected member of the tribe, began his tale.

A long time ago there lived a mighty hero and medicine man named Nanabajou. He was a brave warrior, a skilled hunter and was known for his medicinal skills. Indeed, as a secret patron of the Medicine Society, so great was his magic that he could change himself at will into any living creature that suited his fancy. It was well known that at times he employed this secret knowledge to fulfil his selfish whims. In those days, powerful chieftains possessed several wives to satisfy their desires. Nanabajou, the greatest of them all, had ten wives constantly at his beck and call; they were busy all day long cooking and feeding Nanabajou's many children, scraping and tanning hides, and most important, looking after the physical needs of the mighty chieftain. The heavy tasks he imposed on them during the day were nothing compared to the demands he made at night. This tried them all very much and they complained bitterly: "Nanabajou, mighty chieftain, how can we feed you and your many children, make our clothing, and look after our lodges, when you keep us awake night after night?"

These complaints made Nanabajou angry and he decided to show them who was boss. He picked a hair from his scalp and cut it into nine pieces. At night he burned some herbs with each piece of hair and mixed with it a drop of blood from his little finger. By this powerful magic he conceived nine more Nanabajous! And there was no mistaking them—each had the same star-shaped birthmark on the left buttock. All nine promptly proceeded to the lodges of nine of the wives while Nanabajou himself visited the tenth, which meant that Nanabajou did not waste any time in visiting each lodge in turn. This way he stayed with each of his wives all night. In the morning ten sore wives descended upon the lodge where he was still asleep. "Never mind him being a mighty chieftain," they said. "We will wake him up." And they did. Great was their confusion when each one in turn accused Nanabajou of spending the whole night with her alone.

"My women must be mad," retorted Nanabajou and he stalked out of his lodge in mock disgust.

It was a very hot day and he decided to cool himself beside a lake. As he got closer to the lake he heard someone splashing in the water. Cautiously Nanabajou looked out from behind a tree and saw his oldest daughter enjoying herself in the cool waters of the lake. The sight of her surprised him since he had never seen her undressed before. He noticed that she had quite grown up and how beautiful she had become. "She is ready for a man now. But truly no man deserves her more than I! I must keep an eye on her to protect her from all the evil men who live in our village!"

So Nanabajou was sweet and attentive to his oldest daughter. But with his ten wives around him his task was difficult. The more he thought about his daughter, the less he wanted to lie with his wives. When he stopped seeing them entirely, they complained about that too, just as they had complained when he visited them too often. One day he changed himself into a seagull so that he could watch his daughter while she was bathing in the lake. As he swam around the girl his feathers ruffled with excitement—but what could Nanabajou do as a seagull?

So that night he changed himself into a caterpillar and crawled out of his lodge to where the sleeping girl lay. He crept up her leg and belly and lodged himself between her warm breasts. He had just settled down to enjoy his comfortable resting place when the girl woke up, picked him up between her fingers and threw him out of the lodge. In the morning Nanabajou was sore and bruised all over and he limped badly on one leg. "I had a bad fall when I was hunting deer," he told his ten wives. So they all massaged his bruised body, rubbed it with bear grease, wrapped him up in blankets and placed hot stones all around him to keep him warm. In the evening he was sore no more.

That night Nanabajou again discarded his human form, and this time changed himself into a rabbit. He hopped over to his sleeping daughter and woke her up. Seeing such a nice friendly rabbit, she let him snuggle his soft furry body close to her side. He settled himself comfortably on top of her and licked her breasts with his wet pink tongue. He became so excited that

he wanted to hop up and down on the lovely girl—but what could Nanabajou do as a lowly rabbit?

In the morning, while the girl was still asleep, one of Nanabajou's sons spotted the lively rabbit in the lodge. He picked him up by his long ears and prepared to skin him alive for breakfast. Nanabajou just managed to wriggle out of the boy's grasp and escape to his lodge, where once more he assumed his human form. But Nanabajou's head was sore, he had one black eye and his ears were bruised and swollen.

That evening he felt sick and rolled on the ground in great pain, foaming at the mouth, and gradually becoming weaker and weaker. The efforts of all the medicine men from the secret Medicine Society were in vain. They chanted powerful magic songs to counteract the evil curse which had entered Nanabajou's head. They beat on their drums and tried to suck out the sickness from his head with hollow bear bones. But it was all in vain. In a few hours Nanabajou's hands fell limp, his eyes closed, and he breathed his last.

A great wail went up through the whole village. Nanabajou, the hero of them all, was dead. His ten wives cut off their hair to mourn the loss of their chief and lover. They and all of their children and friends went into deep mourning. Nanabajou, dressed in his best buckskin, was wrapped in strips of birch bark and placed on a high scaffold with his hunting equipment and trophies. For four days and four nights his ten weeping wives and all his children, his relatives and friends sat around it. After a time they returned to their lodges, leaving Nanabajou's body alone on the high scaffold.

Several days later some hunters from the village passed the scaffold where Nanabajou's body lay. They were much dismayed to see blood stains on the wooden platform. Nanabajou's buckskin clothing was torn to shreds and his weapons and trophies were scattered everywhere. There were bear tracks on the soft ground. Obviously the mighty chieftain's body had been devoured by man-eating bears.

The hunters rushed back to the village and related the terrible news. The wise medicine man of the secret Medicine Society listened in grave silence. The evil spell that had possessed Nanabajou must have been powerful indeed. No wonder the strongest magic could not protect him from this horrible curse which not only killed his spirit but also mutilated his body.

Several months after Nanabajou's untimely death, a young stranger arrived in the village. He moved with captivating grace. His fine dark features and long jet-black hair contrasted sharply with his white buckskin clothing, the finest buckskin dress the village had ever seen. The handsome stranger requested hospitality for the night. He had travelled from far away. All ten of Nanabajou's widows welcomed him into their lodges. After some hesitation, the stranger accepted the invitation of one of them, the one whose daughter had been the object of Nanabajou's desire.

He was offered choice caribou tongue and liver, served by the widow's oldest daughter. The handsome stranger, although polite and gracious to his hostess, could not take his eyes off the young woman. The girl was aware of the handsome brave's attentive looks and realized that he was completely captivated by her charms. Although not a word was spoken between them, by her subtle gestures she made it perfectly clear that his attentions were not unwelcome. In spite of her apparent composure, she was far from being calm. Her heart pounded and she felt heat and languor in her body whenever she was close to him. Once he had eaten, the stranger thanked the widow but ignored the girl. He stretched his arms, yawned, and retired to a corner of the lodge where he covered himself with fur robes and was soon asleep.

When the moon was at its fullest and the lodge fire was burning low, the widow's youngest boy woke up and felt an urge to relieve himself. The boy opened the skin-flap door and went outside. When he returned, he heard a strange commotion from where his sister lay. He tiptoed to her side to investigate. He was surprised to see the young stranger wrestling with his sister and holding her down. She was sighing and crying as the stranger was smacking her exposed bottom. The boy was amazed to see that in spite of all this rough treatment, the girl groaned as if in pleasure, embraced the stranger, and spoke to him in endearing terms.

The boy ran to his mother, woke her up, and whispered urgently in her ear, "Come with me and look at my sister! The stranger is beating her—she must have made him very angry for him to act so roughly." Nanabajou's widow hurried to investigate. She could barely make out her oldest daughter, but there, bathed in the full moonlight, she saw the famous bottom with its star-shaped birthmark as it moved up and down! Quietly she left the heaving, sighing couple and called the other wives. They armed themselves with clubs and surrounded Nanabajou. All at once they let out a yell that startled him from his bliss. Before he could collect his wits they whacked him with the clubs until he was bruised and swollen from their blows.

Nanabajou barely managed to escape into the woods. He did not have a stitch of clothing and he shivered with the cold.

"That such a thing should happen to me, the mighty chieftain," he said to himself in sorrow. "Who would have imagined it. Why, I almost came to grief. Those wild women nearly clubbed me to death."

And with these words Nanabajou, cold and sore, disappeared into the forest.

The Evil Indian
and the
Orphan Girl

After hearing of Nanabajou's misfortune, the men in the sweat lodge rocked with laughter. Nanabajou! They had heard many wonderful stories of Nanabajou before, tales which brought back happy memories of their people. Soon they would be heard no more.

It was then that One Eye, an old and respected member of the tribe, placed some sweet-smelling herbs on the hot stones. The fragrant steam spiralled up towards the ceiling and enveloped the perspiring bodies. Their spirits soared skywards with it and the Indians felt light-hearted and gay. Relaxed and comfortable, they listened to One Eye as he told them his story.

A long, long time ago there lived an evil Indian. He took little girls from the villages, hid them in his cabin in the woods, and kept them there until they were almost grown up. Then he abused them and treated them badly. Afterwards they were seen no more.

One day this evil Indian, disguised as a woman, met a young orphan girl in the village. She was about eight or ten years old at that time. The man said to the orphan girl, "Let's go into the woods and hunt for porcupines. Afterwards we will build a fire and have a feast." The orphan girl agreed and they left the village, heading deep into the woods. Sure enough they saw a porcupine in a tree. The Indian climbed up the tree to knock the porcupine down with a club. Just as he was ready to swing his club, the branch broke and he fell to the ground, exposing his buttocks and private parts. The orphan girl realized that she had been fooled: this was not an old woman but a bad man who had tricked her away from her village.

He asked, "What did you see when I fell down?"

"A porcupine up in the tree," she said.

"Did you see anything else?"

"No," she said, "I was staring up at the tree all the time."

They travelled in the woods for many hours until they reached his cabin. Inside was a young Indian girl who gave them some food. The girl was kind to the little orphan but did not speak to her; she seemed sad and afraid.

That night the man and the young girl retired to one side of the lodge and the little orphan girl went to sleep in the opposite corner. At midnight she was wakened by sounds of scuffling, moans, and piteous cries from the young girl. The Indian was abusing her badly; it seemed as if he was beating her and that she was struggling to get away. Then the sounds of struggle ceased and everything was quiet. The orphan girl lay awake and soon she heard something heavy being dragged along the cabin floor. She made out the dim outline of the Indian, bent over and panting with exertion. After a while he left the cabin, and the orphan girl, too frightened to move, pretended to be fast asleep when she heard him come back.

In the morning there was just the two of them. The orphan girl asked, "Where is the girl?"

"She was lonesome for her people," he replied, "and early this morning she went to visit them in the village."

Some time later, the man put a blue bead on the orphan girl's chest. The girl asked him what it was for.

"The bead is there to tell you that you have to marry soon," he said.

"That's curious," answered the orphan girl, "I don't see a man for me to marry."

Since they had not eaten breakfast, the Indian gave her some yellow juice. As soon as she finished it, the girl felt very sleepy. In a little while she was stretched out on her deerskin fast asleep. She must have slept like that for many hours; when she woke up it was already dark. The girl felt strangely different. The buckskin dress did not fit—it was tight all over. She ran her hands over her body. Her chest now shook and rippled every time she moved; her behind was soft and round. Parts of her which were bare only a short time ago were now covered with fine silky hair. The orphan girl, little no longer, rushed to the creek to have a look at herself. To her amazement she saw staring back the reflection of a beautiful woman.

Perturbed, she returned to the cabin; it did not take her long to realize the man's intentions. As she contemplated her fate, she heard his footsteps approaching. Soon it would be too late for her to escape—there was no time to lose. She grabbed her buckskin dress and the bag with the yellow juice, and she rushed out of the cabin quite naked. The Indian saw her and started to run after her, but she was afraid of what he might do to her and ran much faster. Unable to catch up with her, he shouted, "You had better come back to me!" But she did not listen and was soon out of sight.

She ran for hours until, cold and weary, she stopped at a small creek. There she lit a fire, covered herself with her small dress and curled up to go to sleep. It was not too long, however, before she heard the man running towards her, cursing and swearing. The orphan girl quickly pulled some stones out of the fire with a stick. She draped her buckskin dress over them and extinguished the fire so that it looked as if she was sleeping beside the smouldering logs.

The Indian spotted what he thought was the sleeping orphan girl. "I've caught you!" he cried out and exposing his private parts, he jumped at her. His private parts got badly scorched by the hot stones and he yelled in great pain. Enraged, he ran to the creek to cool himself off.

Meanwhile, the girl ran through the forest and found a narrow path which she followed until she came to a spacious lodge. A young hunter lived there all by himself, and when he saw the girl running towards him with not a stitch of clothing on, he was extremely surprised.

"Why have you come this way and why have you no clothing on you?" he asked.

She told him of the evil man who had fooled her, made her grow older, and then wanted to marry her. But she had run away from him since his attentions were most unwelcome.

The young hunter listened to her story and then said, "Never mind, we will fix that man so that he won't bother you any more."

Some time later, they heard shouts outside the lodge. It was the evil man again, still dressed as a woman. He saw the young hunter and said: "My young daughter got lost in the bush, far away from home. I have searched for her all over and I am sure she must have passed this way!"

"Grandmother," said the hunter, "she was here only a while ago. As soon as we finish our meal, my younger brother and I will help you with your search."

With that the man sat down with the two young hunters. He was hungry and tired and suffered badly from his burns. They gave him food and some juice to refresh himself after his long search. He was very thirsty and promptly drank all of the juice. As he drank he aged five years. As he continued drinking he aged another five, and when he finally gulped it all down, he was an old man, his private parts all shrivelled and barely visible.

When the orphan girl saw the evil man aged so much before his time, she laughed.

"We fooled you! From now on you will do no harm to the little girls in the village!"

And as the man stared at her in disbelief, the orphan girl exposed herself, and with great pleasure gave herself to the young hunter. She gave him what the evil man had so greatly desired, but was now too old to enjoy. He watched them in impotent rage as they entwined each other, rocking back and forth with increasing passion. He could not stand it, and, as he was now very old, he doubled over in anguish and died.

29

The
Bear
Walker

O my Grandfather! I am sick and lonely. O Spirit of the sweat bath, heal me. Let my hurt depart upwards like the steam from the sacred stones!"

Thus spoke Big Thunder. There was great sorrow on his face as he addressed the assembled men. His lean and muscular body glistened with sweat. This, however, did not hide the mass of wicked scars that covered his chest.

"You may wish to know," he continued, "how I arrived at this sorry state—I who not long ago was a skilful hunter and enjoyed a woman's love! All this I will tell you, and you, Spirit of the sweat lodge, hear me; restore my spirits and heal me!" And he began his story.

Though my speech is the same as yours, I am a stranger among you. I came from the far North where I lived content and happy with my beautiful woman, Wa-hanata. We had a spacious lodge and all around us were great lakes and forests. We were never short of food or skins for our clothing.

My misfortunes started in the month when all the leaves turn yellow. One day I spotted a herd of caribou not too far from our lodge. Immediately I gave chase, but it was several days before I caught up with them and felled a buck with one shot. With the heavy caribou on my shoulders, I started my journey home.

While I was away in the bush, Wa-hanata decided to go berry-picking. She picked up her birch-bark basket and set off along the path through the bush to a small clearing. There the blackberry bushes grew thick one upon the other, and in no time Wa-hanata had filled her basket full of berries. It was an unusually hot day for that time of year and Wa-hanata, pleasantly tired, settled down on the grass in the clearing and soon fell asleep. In her sleep she had a vision.

She dreamt of a powerful stranger who accosted her on the path in the bush. Although she tried to get away from him she did not succeed, and, as it was no use resisting, Wa-hanata submitted. The stranger exposed himself and covered her with his body. After her initial shock, Wa-hanata reconciled herself to her fate, and, in truth, she enjoyed the stranger's love-making very much.

When she awoke it was already dark, and she realized that she must have been asleep for quite some time. With the memory of the dream still in her mind, Wa-hanata started home. As she approached a large rock, Wa-hanata saw a huge brown bear barring her way. She tried to retrace her steps, but it was too late. The beast had noticed her, and when she backed away he gave a mean growl. Startled and afraid, Wa-hanata stopped, the basket fell from her hand and she stood frozen to the ground. Recovering somewhat, she said to herself: "I must be kind to the bear, and he will let me pass." Slowly she approached the huge animal. She got so close to him that she could feel his hot breath on her face and she became sick and dizzy.

Just the same she addressed the big bear: "O Grandfather, let me show you my affection and then let me go home." As she said this, she gently stroked his neck, his chest and his belly, until she reached his lower parts. She made herself more comfortable by kneeling in front of the bear as, hesitatingly at first, she caressed his genitals. Since he didn't seem to mind, she applied herself to the task with vigour. All at once his body relaxed. He gave a contented sigh and stretched himself on the ground where he lay perfectly still.

"Now," thought Wa-hanata, "this is my chance to escape." Quietly, she got up from her knees and started to creep away. But the big brown bear was not asleep. He opened one eye, gave a mean growl, and with his massive paw beckoned her to come back. Wa-hanata did what she was told. Once more she caressed him and, when she reached his lower parts, the big animal grunted with pleasure.

A strange desire came over Wa-hanata; the spirit of the bear enveloped her senses. She no longer had any thoughts of returning home. As she petted and caressed the great hairy body, the musky odour excited her. Abruptly the bear stood up on his hind legs, seized her in his massive paws and pressed on her with such force that her back bent like a pliant bow. When he covered her, she was totally overcome; she shuddered and moaned in his brute embrace.

When I arrived back at our lodge with the fat caribou buck on my shoulders, Wa-hanata welcomed me in her usual manner but there was no mistaking her air of restlessness and preoccupation. As soon as I had eaten, she told me that she had to pick some blackberries. She combed her hair,

32

put on her best clothes, and stepped out with her basket. When she returned late that evening, the basket was only half full. She was tired and soon went to sleep.

The following morning I asked her, "How is it that you go berry-picking when we have a fat caribou buck and plenty of fish to eat?"

"The berries will be gone soon," she replied, "and I want to dry them for the winter." And then she again put on her best dress, combed her hair, and went out.

As I watched her go, I said to myself, "This is very strange. I'll follow her and see where she goes."

Stealthily I followed her through the bush. There was something about her eagerness that made me curious. I was about twenty paces behind her when she reached a rock not far from the little creek. There she stopped. I hid myself in the bushes, making sure I could see her clearly.

Softly Wa-hanata called, "O my beloved, come out, come out!" To my amazement, a huge brown bear came out from behind the rock and Wa-hanata began to caress his belly and private parts. Then, to my horror, the bear had intercourse with her.

I felt terrible and started to run back to the lodge. On my way I saw a small deer and I killed it with one shot. Instead of returning to the lodge I picked up the deer and carried it to the large rocks at Arrowhead Lake and left it there. Then I hurried home. Soon afterwards Wa-hanata returned. Again she was flushed and tired and soon went to sleep.

The following morning I pretended to be very tired and said to Wa-hanata: "You must go to Arrowhead Lake and get the deer I killed while you were berry-picking." She was reluctant to go, but I insisted.

"All right, I'll go," she said and rushed out of the lodge.

But before she left, she threw a thread of sinew on the fire. It started to shrink and I realized at once that this was Wa-hanata's magic to make the distance between the lodge and Arrowhead Lake shorter. I picked the sinew from the fire, wetted it and stretched it out to its utmost limit.

I took off my clothes and put on one of Wa-hanata's dresses. Then I ran into the bush. When I reached the large rock I called out softly in Wa-hanata's voice.

"My love, come out, come out!" And as the great brown bear emerged from behind the rock, I approached as if to embrace him.

As soon as I was close enough, I plunged my knife deep into his chest. I kept hitting him with my knife again and again, and the great brown bear, realizing that he had been tricked, roared at me with all his fury. He tore at me with his claws and ripped the flesh of my chest and shoulder. Ignoring the burning pain inside me, I kept hitting him desperately with my knife. Blood poured out in great streams and suddenly he keeled over and lay still. I approached him cautiously, and when I saw that he was really dead I cut off his genitals. Then I washed my wounds, dressed them with moss and fern, and started a fire. Over it I roasted the private parts of the bear and ate them, so that I now possessed the power of the bear. Then I hurried back to my lodge.

Late in the evening, Wa-hanata returned home panting with exhaustion.

"I never realized that Arrowhead Lake was so far," she hissed angrily.

"Never mind," I replied, "while I was hunting I hurt my arm. We must rest a few days in the lodge."

The power of the bear was in me and I kept her close to my body for many nights. Wa-hanata seemed to forget the bear and she returned my love with great passion.

One day I told her, "I can't go hunting for a while, my arm is still hurting, but let's go berry-picking to occupy our time." And Wa-hanata, not suspecting anything amiss, agreed.

I led her along the narrow path until we came to the large rock where I killed the great bear. There he lay, stinking and rotting, with maggots and flies crawling all over him.

I grabbed Wa-hanata by the neck and cried out, "There is your great lover! Go and make love to him now!" Still holding her firmly in my grasp, I cut off all her hair. Wa-hanata broke loose, and in the struggle she touched my charm bag. Inside this bag were the testicles of a beaver, the source of my masculine power, and when she touched the bag she destroyed my potency. The spirit of the bear then entered Wa-hanata and she became a bear-walker, at times human, and at times bear-like. Quite lost, she wanders forever like a ghost from one place to another.

Desolate in spirit, I left my lodge. For many days I travelled in an unknown country, where I met many friendly people. They made me welcome in their lodges and their women were very kind to me. But since the curse of Wa-hanata was on me I could not return their kindness, and at night I was always lonely.

This is my story, and now I pray to you, Spirit of this sweat lodge, heal me, and let my hurt depart upwards as does the steam from these sacred stones!

In the silence that followed Big Thunder's story, more water was poured over the heated stones and thick steam spiralled towards the ceiling.

It was then that Blue Sky turned to Big Thunder and said: "My Son, there is sorrow in our hearts, and we have pity for you as your misfortune is great. But the wicked Bear Walker's curse is not final. We can destroy it according to our ancient ways!"

Gravely, Blue Sky threw some red, brown and yellow herbs into the sacred fire. The sweet-smelling herbs burned and the smoke rose and mixed with the thick steam. Big Thunder inhaled the sticky vapour deeply. Soon his body stopped trembling and his weariness passed away. Completely unaware of his surroundings, he stared at the ceiling. There the thick white smoke curled and twisted and assumed fantastic shapes. Out of this swirling mass one shape became clearer than the others; it detached itself from the rest and assumed the form of a girl. Big Thunder knew her. She had looked after him when he first arrived in the village and was kind to him. She would have welcomed his attentions but he was afraid and had avoided her. Now she smiled at him and gently beckoned him on.

Big Thunder was afraid no longer. Bursting with happiness he soared towards the ceiling, and there, in the smoke and steam, he embraced the smiling girl.

Big One
and the
Bad Medicine Woman

The naked men perspired freely as more water was poured over the red-hot stones. Soon the sweat lodge was full of thick white steam which hid their nakedness. Only an occasional murmur was heard in the dark interior. Then the powerful voice of One Eye attracted their attention.

"Brothers, you have just witnessed the sorrow in a man's heart when he could feel himself a man no longer. Indeed, the penis is the staff of life, the very essence of our strength. Wise was the great Manitou when he created man and endowed him with a penis, for he made sure that our dreams would be perpetuated for time without end. Listen to the story of my grandfather, Big One, and of the bad medicine woman who tried to destroy him."

Many, many years ago, my grandfather, Big One, lived in a solitary lodge beside a lake with his parents and his older brother. One day his brother had a talk with his parents.

"I am all by myself here and lonely; the time has come for me to go out into the world and find myself a woman." Once he had informed them of his intentions he packed his possessions into a canoe and slipped a raven's head charm around Big One's neck.

Just before he departed, he took Big One aside and said, "If anything should happen to me the raven's head will give you a sign and you must follow in my steps." And with these words he stepped into his canoe and disappeared from sight. He was gone for many months and nothing more was heard of him.

One night Big One had a vision. In his dream he saw a large black raven carrying a penis in its beak. As it flew over a lake, the raven squawked and the penis dropped out of its beak and disappeared in the water below. The

37

raven dove into the lake as if to retrieve it, but the water rose over the bird and it, too, disappeared from sight.

Big One awoke from his dream with a start. He knew for sure that his brother was dead, and that it was his duty to avenge him. Like his brother before him, he packed his possessions into a canoe, bid his parents goodbye, and departed.

He travelled for many weeks without meeting anyone until he reached a large lake. He was more than happy when he noticed, high up on the shore, a single lodge. He beached his canoe and entered the lodge. Inside he found a beautiful young girl. Tired from his long journey, he asked permission to rest a while. The young girl readily agreed and welcomed him to stay with her.

During the night, Big One felt a movement at his side. It was the young girl. She touched his cheek and gently caressed his body. Big One felt strange—he had never felt like this before. His confusion increased when the girl placed her body on top of his. Big One, uninitiated in the ways of love, did not know what to do with himself. As the young girl continued her caresses, Big One suddenly acquired an extra leg! Or so it seemed to him. This third leg was awkward and kept getting in the way between him and the lovely girl. He really didn't know what to do with it, and in fact, was quite ashamed of it. Suddenly the girl, who was still on top of him, knelt forward in such a manner that his third leg disappeared from sight. The girl had swallowed it! She continued with her caresses and soon Big One was shuddering with pleasure. He quickly became proficient at his task, and applied himself with great vigour.

It became obvious that his name, Big One, had not been given to him without reason. In fact his third leg was the largest one the girl had ever known. She became completely enamoured of him and of his extra leg, which both of them put to good use.

The young girl really loved the boy. She waited upon him, anticipated his wishes, and fed him the choicest foods. Big One, quite comfortable in the lodge, forgot his mission and spent happy nights and days with the girl instead.

One day, as the two of them were making love, there was a commotion outside the lodge. The door flew open and a young woman, the girl's sister, walked in. She was the most beautiful creature that Big One had ever seen. Hastily, he disengaged himself from his companion and gaped open-mouthed at the new girl. In no time Big One had become completely obsessed with this beautiful woman and had fallen madly in love with her. However, in order not to hurt the younger girl's feelings, Big One played a waiting game. But he could not hide his intentions. Whenever she moved around the lodge he followed her with his eyes, obeyed her slightest whim, and brought her food and water. He was constantly at her beck and call. His loss of interest in the younger sister did not remain unnoticed for long. The young girl, desolate and unhappy, berated him for his lack of attention, but he didn't listen.

Finally, exasperated, she burst out, "My sister is an evil witch and when you make love to her she will destroy you!"

Big One payed no attention, but said to himself, "The girl is jealous, she's only trying to put me off; I will have no more dealings with her."

One day when the young girl was away from the lodge, he said to her sister, "This is a fine day for fishing; let's go and fish together." She agreed, and they went off in a canoe and caught many fish. When they were a long way from the shore, Big One remembered that he had seen this lake before, but since that lovely girl was with him he didn't give it much thought.

Suddenly, without warning, the lake, which had been smooth and quiet, started to boil. Tremendous waves sprang out of nowhere and the little canoe was tossed up and down in the turbulent waters. Yet, strangely, there was no wind and the sun shone brightly in the sky. The spirits of the raven and of his brother's penis were trying to warn him but Big One, enamoured of the girl beside him, did not understand. He had great difficulty keeping his balance in the little canoe; he was tossed from side to side and nearly overturned, but he was surprised to see his companion sitting upright and comfortable. Even the strongest waves failed to move her from her seat. With great effort, Big One paddled the canoe back to safety. As he beached it he looked at the plank where the girl had been seated. He was amazed to see holes in the centre of the plank as if spikes had been driven through it. He thought this was very strange until he recalled her sister's warning and recognized the lake from his dream. He cursed himself for his folly.

He sat down beside her and gently took her in his arms. "Let me feel you," he whispered in her ear. The girl agreed, and soon she lay naked on the ground. Big One caressed her body until the girl was flushed and panted heavily with desire. He knelt over her, and when she closed her eyes, ready to receive him, he grabbed the paddle and shoved the handle deep inside her. He heard a horrible crunching noise, and when he withdrew it, teeth fell out of her private parts. In a rage she screamed at him, but he had her firmly by the throat. Now he knew that with those teeth she had intended to kill him the way she had killed his brother. Big One picked up a rock and smashed the skull of the bad medicine woman who copulated with men and killed them with the teeth in her vagina.

He returned to the lodge of the young girl who really loved him and stayed with her for many years. They had a daughter. One day, Big One was sitting with his wife and daughter by the fire cracking nuts when suddenly the little girl picked up a nut and pushed it inside her. There was a loud crunching noise and the nut was broken. Stunned, Big One watched the little girl without a word. Again she picked up a nut and pushed it inside; Big One looked there and saw a row of sharp little teeth in her vagina. He did not hesitate. He picked up a large rock and crushed her skull. The curse of the bad medicine woman was upon his little girl too.

"All that happened a long time ago. Since then times have changed and things are very different," said One Eye as he concluded his story. "But, brothers, you had better remember this—there are many enemies of man who try to deprive him of his power."

The
Medicine
Dream

As One Eye concluded his tale of the bad medicine woman who had met her just fate, the assembled men nodded their heads in approval. They were very proud of their organs and of the power that had been given to them by the Great Provider. They were therefore surprised when a dissenting voice was heard from the back of the sweat lodge not far from the door. It belonged to Dark Cloud.

"One Eye, wise man of our people, I respect your opinion. What you say is true—the penis is indeed the strength of man. But in fact, when you think about it, its strength is small and doesn't last long once it is swallowed up by a woman. It soon wears out. The penis is really a bare-faced liar as it struts and threatens all blown up with pride. But it soon finds out to its sorrow that a woman's private part is like a bottomless pot. It can be filled only for a short time; most of the time the pot stays empty. It's like a dense forest: you can shoot it full of arrows; the arrows get lost in the underbrush but the forest remains the same. You don't believe me? I see puzzlement in your eyes and doubt on your faces. Brothers, may the spirit of the sacred lodge teach you wisdom. I will tell you the story of my grandfather, Short Arrow, as it was told to me a long time ago. So listen to what I have to say."

It was in the month of berries that Short Arrow had a dream. In his dream he had a vision of a lovely girl sitting beside a rock, gazing intently at a fast-flowing stream. Short Arrow watched the beautiful girl, until she, becoming aware of his scrutiny, lifted her head and looked him straight in the face. Short Arrow was seized with great desire and his heart pounded wildly as he advanced towards the girl. The girl reached out to him, caressed and fondled him until his penis became big and swollen.

He was just about to cover her when suddenly there was a loud thunderclap and both of them jumped in surprise. In the distance they heard the steady beat of a drum. All at once the girl and Short Arrow were surrounded by a dozen young braves. They promptly exposed their private parts and moved towards the girl. Confused at the unexpected intrusion, the girl stopped caressing Short Arrow and looked around at the braves.

She turned away from Short Arrow and reached for the brave nearest to her. She fondled his private parts and soon he too was very excited. As soon as he was ready to cover her, she twisted away from him and touched another brave. He became aroused, but already she was fondling the exposed parts of yet another brave. Soon all the braves were excited and pushed so near that they were touching her with their organs and she could hardly move. There was no mistaking the girl's desire; her hand flew from one brave to another. She caressed them, played with their private parts and then withdrew in indecision. All at once her hesitation vanished. She grasped Short Arrow firmly by the waist and pulled him to the ground. Then the sound of the drum stopped and the young braves suddenly disappeared. Short Arrow promptly covered the girl and had intercourse with her.

After a while he awoke from his dream but the vision of the beautiful young girl would not leave him. He thought of her so often that she became quite real in his mind.

Several moons later, Short Arrow was travelling in a strange country, far from home. He walked along a narrow pathway in the forest and eventually came to a clearing with several lodges beside a small river. Short Arrow entered the settlement and was soon surrounded by curious people. As he approached the lodge nearest the river he recognized the rock where he had seen the girl in his dream. Short Arrow approached the rock and his heart leapt with joy when he saw her sitting beside the rock. She smiled in greeting and at once, invited him to her lodge. Short Arrow was again consumed with great passion for her. She seemed to anticipate all his wishes and very soon Short Arrow and the girl exposed themselves to each other. From his vision Short Arrow already knew her smallest gestures and most intimate details. And she seemed more than familiar with him. She caressed and fondled him until Short Arrow, swollen with desire, seized the only-too-willing girl and possessed her.

After some time, he rested beside her, and, still puzzled by her unexpected willingness to satisfy his desire, he said: "How is it you act as if you have known me for a long time and yet I am a stranger in this country?"

The girl replied: "It was several moons ago in the month of berries that I went to the big rock beside the river to pray and meditate. For several days I had no food or water and I hoped for a medicine dream to guide me and to purify my soul. I dreamed I saw a large bag floating down the river. I was happy to see it as I was sure it was a medicinal bag sent to me by my dream spirit. I hurried to pull it from the river, and I untied the cords eagerly. Great was my surprise when I found that it was full of male private parts. I pulled them out from the bag and spread them on the grass. There must have been at least a dozen—all sizes and shapes. They were all so lovely that I ran my hands from one to the other and every time I put my hands on one it came to life and became big and swollen. They looked so beautiful that I wanted them all. I was hot and restless and finally I could wait no more, so I picked up the one nearest to me and had intercourse with it. I never expected to have such powerful medicine inside of me! However, the penis soon tired and, to my dismay, lost its medicinal power. I moved to the next one—a really big one, and when I caressed it, it got bigger still and soon, deep inside me, it released its medicinal power and set me all on fire. After a time it shrank too, and left me. But there were more. And so with great pleasure I spent the whole day. I moved from one penis to another, fondling, caressing and having intercourse with them. With all that pleasant exercise I was flushed and tired. Never had I achieved such contentment before; the medicine that I discovered in my dream was certainly powerful. It gave me strength and uplifted my soul. Towards the end of the day I approached the only male organ that I had not yet had intercourse with. All the others were stretched out limply on the ground. The last one was not a particularly big one but it was not small either; it was about medium size, and when I stroked it with my fingers it shot up with great spirit and proceeded to have intercourse with me. And as I experienced its powers, I wished that I could keep this one with me forever. Then I awoke from my dream.

"And so it was foretold in my dreams that you would come here and that you would possess me. I recognized you at once and your penis is not exactly unknown to me. It is my wish to hold on to it forever."

When the girl had finished, Short Arrow was perplexed. It was true that he had recognized her at once from his dream and that he had had intercourse with her in his vision. And yet in his dream he had been the only one to gain her favours. That apparently was not the case. However, she had chosen him above all the others. His doubts vanished as once more he felt her soft hands fondling and caressing those places that pleased him most. When her body entwined with his he forgot all about dreams. The following day they travelled to his lodge.

He was most happy with the beautiful young woman who was now his wife, and he did not leave his lodge for many weeks. He abandoned his trap line and shied away from friends, staying with her night and day. And so his larder became empty and his medicine bag lost its power. With nothing but berries in his belly there was little fuel to rekindle his fire. When he was next to his young wife sleep was his greatest desire. Her nakedness did not excite him. With all her love and caresses his private parts remained no bigger than before.

"How is it," she said to him angrily, "that you are so small and tired all the time and have no medicine in your bag when in our dreams you treated me so well?" Wearily he tried to please her, but with no more arrows in his bag, he turned over and was soon asleep. He woke up early, and stealthily, so as not to wake his wife, he stole away from the lodge. He rejoined his friends in the bush and once more felt the excitement of the chase. He hunted, gossiped, gambled, and enjoyed the male companionship of his friends.

One night he had a dream in which he saw his lodge and his young wife inside. There were twelve young braves all around her, their private parts fully exposed. His wife caressed them all. In the distance he heard the savage pounding of a drum as the young braves ran around her in a tight circle with cries of lustful frenzy. They forced her to the ground and took her one by one.

With cold sweat on his brow, Short Arrow woke up and hurried at once to his lodge. When he arrived he was surprised to see his young wife content and happy. He noticed that their larder held an abundance of meat and provisions and a large woodpile stood outside the lodge. He asked how she had managed to get the supplies all by herself.

"I had a few relatives who visited me from my village and they brought me these gifts," she answered. Short Arrow did not tell her of his vision but decided to stay close to home.

After his stay in the bush, he was well fed and rested, and full of that medicinal power the young woman so constantly required. He remained in that happy state for a number of sleeps, but sooner than he had expected, his bag was empty and the girl was again very unhappy with Short Arrow.

Frustrated, he rejoined his friends in the bush and there he hunted, fished and enjoyed their company. But he didn't remain in that carefree state for long. He had another dream about his young wife. She was naked and surrounded by the twelve young braves. Ghost-like, they circled slowly around her, their steps keeping time to the beat of a distant drum. As they moved around her, she fondled their organs. In no time she became very excited; her hands flew swiftly from one organ to another until they became enormously swollen. The braves kept her in a tight circle and as the drum started to beat faster and faster they danced around her with increasing frenzy. To the savage beating of the drum they pulled her to the ground, and one by one had intercourse with her.

Alarmed, Short Arrow awoke from his dream and hastened back to his lodge. There he found his wife content and happy, and as before, there was a supply of fresh food in the larder. He made no reference to his dream but determined to stay with her all the time.

Short Arrow stayed in his lodge for a long time and, when the food was gone, he picked berries from the bush and trapped rabbits close to home. He refused to leave her alone. And when once again he had no power in his

bag, both of them were unhappy and frustrated. In spite of their bitterness he would not leave her. In desperation he sought the advice of Red Stones, the medicine man, and found him in the sweat lodge.

As Short Arrow entered the steamy interior he pleaded with the medicine man: "May the spirit of this sweat lodge have pity on me, and you Red Stones, advise me! How can I fight the evil spirit of the medicine bag that has possessed my wife? No matter how great a man's power is it soon wears out when in contact with a woman." Short Arrow told the story of his misfortune, and the medicine man listened with great attention. When Short Arrow finished, the steam hissed and spiralled upwards from the red-hot stones. The medicine man was enveloped in a cloud of vapour and could be seen no more. Then he addressed Short Arrow.

"My son, great indeed is your misfortune. The medicine bag your wife saw in her vision has tried you sorely. But our dreams and visions are true, and we must obey them. This is the will of the great master of life. Your vision has told you that only you should have her as a wife. And it is only because of this that I may be able to help you. At full moon, your wife will have another dream. But this time I will arrange it so that you will dream with her and your visions will coincide. Drink the mushroom juice that you will find at the door of this lodge before you retire. It will be for the great master of life to decide what will happen in your dreams."

Short Arrow thanked the medicine man. He found the mushroom juice and returned to his wife. At full moon he drank all the mushroom juice given to him by the medicine man, and fell fast asleep. In his dreams he found himself outside his lodge. The moon was still high in the sky. Suddenly he heard some footsteps, followed by the low beating of a drum. He flattened himself on the ground. In the full moonlight he saw the twelve young braves, marching in single file, enter his lodge. Cautiously he followed them and peeped through the door. He saw his wife, fully exposed, breathing heavily and surrounded by the braves who were all extremely aroused. Suddenly the sound of the drum changed. It started to pound wildly right behind the hiding man and, just as the braves pulled the woman down, Short Arrow leapt in and with a blood-curdling yell attacked them with his knife. His arm flew swiftly from one startled man to another. Covered with sweat and blood he killed them all, cut off their organs and threw them to the ground. Still frenzied by the pounding of the drum and gripped by an overpowering rage, he advanced on his wife. He possessed her as he never had before. And as their bodies tensed and arched and were about to explode, Short Arrow gave a triumphant cry. The drum beat slowed; its sounds grew softer until finally it died away.

In the peace that followed, he was delivered from his past sorrows and thereafter drifted only in the world of gentler dreams.

The
Magic
Gun

The sky became overcast. Dark clouds propelled by a furious wind rolled up from the east accompanied by loud claps of thunder and flashes of light in the distance.

Under the darkened sky the sweat lodge disappeared from sight and, as the storm raged outside and a host of demons and evil spirits galloped madly across the sky, the men like mute sentinels sat around the sacred stones; light shimmered on their sweaty faces, and ghostlike shadows danced inside the lodge, while they, suspended between the world of the living and the world of the dead, waited in the eerie silence. It was broken by True Blood, a much respected elder of the tribe.

"Hear now my brothers, this is a strange night; the lodge has put a spell on us. We talk of our women and the intimate details of our lives, the very things that we are usually most reluctant to discuss. Yes, these sacred stones reveal the secrets buried in our hearts, so let it be. Listen to my tale."

It all started in our settlement a hundred years ago when my grandparents were still young. One summer evening a stranger was seen emerging from the forest following the pathway towards the centre of the village. He passed a group of young women who were cheerfully busy tanning hides. They exchanged friendly greetings. From the distance he heard the dogs barking and when he approached the open plain, he saw around him many spacious lodges with fires blazing and women looking after the cooking. On the shore of the river, children were playing among the birch-bark canoes. Soon the stranger was surrounded by a group of friendly people and was welcomed by the chief of the settlement. They fed him well, and put him up for the night.

The stranger's name was Dancing Light. Although he had never travelled in these parts, the people had heard of him. He had a reputation as a skilful carver and a great storyteller. He made ceremonial masks and vessels, pipes, charms, and toys, which he coloured with red or yellow ochre and paints extracted from plants, herbs and berries. He specialized in stories about the demons, ghosts, and spirits that dwelt in trees, mountain-tops and rivers. He was always happy and had a kind disposition and, although some Indian braves looked down on him because he would not join in their manly ventures, he did not seem to mind. He was quite content to live in his own way. His parents long since dead, he was all by himself and spent his time travelling from one settlement to another where he stayed as long as his services were required.

Tired after his long journey, he did not wake up until late the following day. Most of the men were already in the bush hunting and the women were busy working around the lodges when he strolled towards the river to bathe. Afterwards he perched himself on a rock and, soon surrounded by a group of eager children, told stories of days gone by. Just as he was telling them of the gruesome fight between Big Goose and the evil Windigo, he heard a noise not far along the river bank.

He looked up to see a slender young woman in a fringed deerskin dress carrying a birch-bark bucket. She stooped down at the river's edge and filled her bucket. Then she retraced her steps and disappeared among the lodges. Dancing Light followed her with his eyes until she was gone. Although he had seen her for only a moment, he was completely captivated by her beauty. Her soft, full face was framed by long raven hair pulled back tightly at the nape of her neck and draped across one shoulder. She moved with easy grace and, although her dark eyes were serious, he sensed gaiety and laughter beneath them.

Dancing Light hurriedly finished his story, much to the disappointment of his audience, and he strode casually past the lodges exchanging friendly greetings with his new neighbours. It did not take him long to find out that the young woman was a widow. Her husband had recently been killed in a fight, the nature of which his neighbours were reluctant to discuss.

The young widow soon became aware of the stranger's interest in her. Whether he was telling a story or carving something out of wood, his eyes followed her, watching her slightest movement, obviously disappointed when she was out of sight. He always managed to be near enough to make his presence felt. It disturbed her and made her weak inside. Without a word the two reached complete understanding. The villagers noticed it, but did not make any comment on something which was, after all, a very personal affair.

It was no surprise to them that one day Dancing Light gathered his possessions and moved into the young widow's lodge. And if the braves silently reproached him with their stares for not joining them in their exploits, Dancing Light did not mind. He had no intention of leaving this loving woman even for a single night. He was constantly aware of his wife's affection, even when he was with other people, carving or storytelling. The way she looked at him and her tender, subtle gestures set his blood on fire. At times, the two of them would fish in the lake or walk deep into the forest in search of the roots and berries he needed for his paints.

One day, as they were walking in the woods, they found a small blue lake full of trout and they often returned there. They pitched a skin tent near the shore and fished in the lake, gathered berries in the bush, and set snares for small game. On hot summer nights they slept under the stars. At times the urgent cravings of their bodies sent them in search of each other. Afterwards they regarded each other with tenderness and wonder, their happiness complete. They spoke very little and yet always seemed to anticipate each other's wishes. Their lives were filled with great peace and contentment.

Dancing Light was surprised one day when, stepping outside the lodge, he saw a small skin tent pitched right in front of his door. Near it, beside a campfire, sat a stranger who greeted him politely. Dancing Light returned the greeting and made his way towards the river. With all the empty space around, Dancing Light found it difficult to understand the stranger's reason for setting himself down right beside his door. However, it was not his business to interfere with the stranger's whim, so he thought of it no more.

But he was more than surprised when the following day he noted two more tents pitched right outside his lodge! There were several strangers nearby and they all gave him a polite greeting. Dancing Light did not know what to make of their peculiar behaviour and the next day he was astounded to see six more tents around his lodge. They were full of strangers, who, on seeing him, greeted him courteously. It seemed as if they were waiting for him. But since they apparently did not wish to state the nature of their visit Dancing Light was not going to ask them.

That evening, puzzled and annoyed at this unexpected intrusion, he asked his wife, "Why have these strangers decided to set themselves down right on our front door and disturb our privacy when there is all that empty land in and around the village?"

He was startled by her reply. "It grieves me to tell you that my dead husband was a gambler and that he owed these people many things, all lost in games of chance. In fact, he was killed by one of them while cheating."

Suddenly Dancing Light realized his predicament. He knew that, according to ancient Indian law, no man would ever press a widow for her late husband's debts. Once she remarried, however, it was a different matter. Her new husband was expected to take over her obligations, including those of the dead husband. Bewildered by this unexpected turn of events, Dancing Light went outside. He greeted the assembled strangers, sat down beside them and they passed the pipe around. Gravely they told him of his obligations—an incredible number. He owed muskets, iron pots, buffalo robes, tobacco, and many beaver pelts! Dancing Light took note of the many things that his wife's first husband had gambled away, and promising to give the matter his urgent consideration, retired to his lodge to think.

When he woke up the following morning, he was amazed to see, pitched right outside his door, yet another tent. Dancing Light went out to investigate. It belonged to Crooked Mouth. In spite of his unattractive appearance—his skin pocked by disease, a bad limp, a twisted mouth and, when he laughed, an eye which rolled upwards in his head—Crooked Mouth was a great hunter, and because of his skill, very wealthy. He owned several horses, many muskets, buffalo robes, and piles of beaver pelts.

He stated the purpose of his visit: "It has been said the young widow has remarried. I, too, have come to collect my debts: one musket, three buffalo robes and ten beaver pelts." In the silence that followed, Dancing Light gravely puffed at his pipe, not knowing what to say.

Crooked Mouth addressed him once more: "For many months I've been hunting, and have many skins, furs and muskets. However, all that time I was without a woman, and now I feel my need quite urgent. It may surprise you, but I wish to have your wife. In fact, I wanted her before she married that gambler who tried to cheat me in the moccasin game. For once I was too late. Be that as it may, right now I would like to trade with you. I'll pay off your obligations to all those people who are assembled round your place, and I'll forget the musket, beaver pelts and buffalo robes you owe me. But I will take your wife in trade. I will even give you one musket and some choice beaver pelts." Dancing Light realized that Crooked Mouth, inflamed with passion for his young wife, had indeed made him a generous offer. But he was happy with her, and would not let her go.

"No," was his reply, "my woman stays with me! I'll go north and like you I'll kill game." On hearing these words, Crooked Mouth laughed so hard that his eye rolled upwards and disappeared into his head.

Undaunted, and equipped with a spear, bow and arrows, Dancing Light set out for the north country to hunt for furs. But not being a skilled hunter, he had little success, and returned several moons later, exhausted, empty-handed and resigned to his fate. Miserable, he avoided his wife's unhappy gaze.

News of his return spread all around the lodges, and sooner than he expected, he was confronted by Crooked Mouth. Quietly Dancing Light addressed him: "So let it be. My woman now belongs to you. She is yours for all the things that I owe to you and to the other people." His wife could not very well argue since it was because of her that he had been forced to do this. The only honourable thing for her to do was to submit to Crooked Mouth's will. Crooked Mouth did not waste any time and soon he was back laden with beaver pelts, buffalo robes and muskets. He pulled the young woman to her feet and curtly told her that she was now his and must follow him. And while Dancing Light, resigned to his loss, puffed at his pipe, she left with Crooked Mouth.

Dancing Light tried to console himself with the thought that one woman was as good as another, and that in the settlement there were quite a number available. He was now a rich man and finding another wife would not be difficult. Sure enough it did not take any time at all for the villagers to learn of the exchange and the fact that Dancing Light was on the lookout for another wife. All the unmarried girls were extremely willing and, as he was lonely, he tried one woman after another. But it was no use. It was not the same; he could not stop thinking of his wife and his gestures were empty.

Meanwhile, Crooked Mouth, after satisfying his passion, did not find his life agreeable either. His new wife was sullen and morose. She never laughed at his sly jokes and, what was even worse, she never praised him for being a great hunter, which indeed he was. Obediently she did what he asked of her but no more, and, contrary to his expectations, she was cold and did not respond to his embraces. He began to regret the folly that led him to such a foolish exchange. Furthermore, he envied Dancing Light who had the pick of all the young women in the village. He watched bitterly as Dancing Light tried them all, one by one, and was even more incensed when, still undecided, Dancing Light started on his second round. He was convinced that Dancing Light was only having fun and had no serious intention to marry. However, Crooked Mouth could not very well admit to having made a foolish trade; that would make him the laughing stock of the village. So he pretended to be perfectly content with his wife.

But Dancing Light was not easily fooled. He soon realized that Crooked Mouth was not happy. And although she never complained or even looked at her former husband, Dancing Light knew that his beloved missed him too and that her heart was heavy.

One day he overheard several braves in a conversation. They were all excited and kept referring to the Wahn-chesta gun, a truly magic gun, that could fire seven times in quick succession without reloading. Hunting with the magic gun was very easy. The braves had seen it at the trading post of the white man, but it cost so much that it was far beyond their means. Dancing Light digested the news and the following day visited Crooked Mouth's lodge.

After they had exchanged greetings, Dancing Light said: "Crooked Mouth, how is it that I see nothing in your lodge but a few old-fashioned muskets, spears, and bows and arrows? For a great hunter, your equipment is obsolete. Why don't you have the Wahn-chesta gun, the magic gun that fires seven times without reloading? A gun like that would spread your fame right across this land!" Crooked Mouth solemnly agreed that he would indeed be very happy to own such a magic gun.

"Now it's my turn to propose a trade," said Dancing Light. "If you promise me the woman, I'll get you the magic gun." And Crooked Mouth, fed up to the teeth with the cold and sulky woman, was only too happy to agree.

Dancing Light picked up his musket and his precious bundle of beaver pelts and set off for the trading post. Somehow he would get that magic gun from the whites. The trading post was not that far from his settlement, and he reached it within a few hours.

The sun shone brightly over the tree tops when Dancing Light emerged from the forest. Here the trail ended, and the narrow pathway disappeared in an outcropping of mossy boulders and thick patches of scrub and grass. Ahead of him, where the rocky ground sloped down gently to a large field, he saw two large log buildings surrounded by a high wooden fence. On the plain, clustered on one side of the fence, was an Indian encampment. At the moment most of its occupants, men, women and children, mingled together in front of the large gate leading to the trading post.

Dancing Light was surprised by the peculiar behaviour of the crowd. These usually silent and reticent people were now singing, crying or quarrelling loudly with each other. They looked as if they all had been possessed by an evil spirit. The men paraded in grotesque costumes of all shapes and colours: fancy broadbrimmed hats with tall feathers, multicoloured vests, trousers, and knee-high boots. Some wore the full dress of wagoners, women or sailors. The women were dressed in calico gowns, buttonless vests, flannel coats and stove-pipe hats.

With difficulty Dancing Light pushed his way through the jostling crowd, past the stout gate in the fence and entered one of the log houses. There he came face to face with a small evil-looking man dressed in black. Very fat, his scalp was pink and bare, and curly black hair stood out all over his face. He looked like a creature from a bad dream. Scared, Dancing Light wanted to turn back, but the evil-looking man, noticing the bundle of pelts, grabbed him by the arm and spoke to someone in the room.

It was then that Dancing Light noticed another Indian. The Indian spoke the language of the white man. So Dancing Light stated the purpose of his visit: "A Wahn-chesta gun is wanted." When told of his wishes, the white man laughed out loud, and, sure enough, from behind the counter produced the gun. Dancing Light looked at it with awe. Never before had he seen such a small gun! It looked like a toy. He picked it up and chanted a protective song to propitiate the great spirit of the magic gun. He stood it upright on the floor, and, according to the time-honoured formula, picked up his beaver pelts, one by one, until they stood level with the muzzle of the magic gun. He offered them to the white trader, but the latter pushed them away. His assistant called Dancing Light an ignorant Indian.

"For that Wahn-chesta gun, which fires seven times without reloading, you'll have to give the trader seven times as many beaver pelts. But, since you've come so far, the trader will be happy to oblige you with some of his firewater for all your pelts." Dancing Light stubbornly repeated that he wanted only the Wahn-chesta gun, and this so exasperated the white trader that he kicked him out of the store.

Outside, not knowing where to go, Dancing Light mingled with the crowd. It surprised him to see some men obviously weak and emaciated with hunger, and yet not far away the forests, lakes and rivers teemed with fish, game and enough to satisfy all their needs. A number of women and children were sick and were covered with rags and filth. Bewildered, he followed these people until he came to the second log building.

There, surrounded by a crowd of attentive Indians, he saw two white people, the sons of the trader. They were filling up small crocks with something from a large barrel that looked like water. While the crowd watched spellbound, a weak and emaciated Indian pushed through the crowd and accosted the white men. Behind him were his wife and their young daughter. The Indian offered his wife in trade for some of the magic water. The trader's eldest son looked the woman over, and, finding her still young and attractive, accepted her husband's offer. He gave him a mugful of the water for the wife and the daughter. He pushed the girl towards his brother while he, surrounded by the wildly cheering crowd, undressed the wife and sported with her in the open field. Meanwhile the husband consumed the magic water, not paying the slightest attention to the trader's son having such fun with his wife.

Once it was over, the trader's son pushed her aside and directed his attention to his brother. Aroused by the spectacle of his brother's behaviour with the wife, the younger son proceeded to do likewise with the girl. But it was his first experience of this kind. The small girl lay exposed beneath him, confused and frightened by all the shouting from the crowd. The boy tried and sweated, but all at once desire left him. Flushed and humiliated, he pushed his way through the jeering mob and disappeared from sight.

The trader's eldest son, furious at what was happening, determined to show the Indians that a deal must be paid in full! The girl's small body writhed and twisted frantically on the ground as he pressed down on her with his gross black-haired belly. She did not scream but closed her eyes. As the searing pain ripped her apart and bit deep into her, she fainted. Satisfied, the trader's son let go of her. The crowd of onlookers dispersed, leaving the limp girl alone in the field. It sickened Dancing Light and he walked away in disgust.

Dusk was already settling over the encampment and fires were being lit, when he stumbled across a group of silent men. Cross-legged, they sat in a semicircle watching the moccasin game. In the centre of the crowd two men sat on a buffalo skin facing each other. One of the men, wearing a tall beaver hat and a red sash across his naked chest, had a deep scar across his face.

In the red glow of the flame he looked quite evil. Beside him was an enormous pile of beaver pelts. His opponent, dressed only in a pair of leather britches, was not faring well. He had only four pelts left.

It was the latter's turn to hide the musket ball under one of the four moccasins placed between the players. He took the ball between his thumb and two fingers and then, with great dexterity began to shuffle his hand under the first, second, third and fourth moccasins. All the time he hummed his gambling song. The song stopped. The hand withdrew, empty. Now it was Scarface's turn to find the hidden ball. The crowd watched intently as Scarface, resplendent in his tall beaver hat, stood up. After invoking the deities, he hesitated only a fraction of a second before making his choice. A lift! And there under the moccasin was the hidden ball. A deep sigh went through the crowd. He had won the four remaining beaver pelts. He surveyed the crowd of onlookers, but no one dared to face him in the moccasin game.

Suddenly he saw Dancing Light clinging to his bundle of furs and immediately challenged him. Dancing Light, desperate for a treasure of beaver pelts, accepted his challenge. Cross-legged they sat on the buffalo skin facing each other. The game went on through the best part of the night. Luck shifted between them, but at length it began to favour Dancing Light—pelts began to accumulate on his pile while that of his opponent grew progressively smaller. The game continued until at last Scarface's last pelt was gone. In a fit of desperation he staked his musket. That too was lost. Perspiration stood upon his brow and frantic, he staked his wife. But Dancing Light stoutly refused. His opponent insisted, becoming indignant and using offensive language. And when Dancing Light still would not accept his challenge, Scarface sprang to his feet and attacked him with a knife. Dancing Light saw it coming and quickly rolled out of his reach. The crowd disarmed the attacker, who disappeared into the darkness.

Dancing Light fastened his enormous pile of beaver pelts with rawhide and waited until daybreak for the trading post to open. Happily, he confronted the white trader.

"A magic gun is still wanted," he said, pushing forward his enormous bundle of furs. The white trader beamed and from under the counter produced the magic gun and handed it to the happy Indian.

Just as Dancing Light was about to leave, the trader barred his way and, through his interpreter, said to him: "We whites have a custom which is never broken. When trade is concluded we toast each other with magic water."

Dancing Light was only too happy to oblige. He waited while the trader filled two large mugs and handed one to him. It was firewater! He had some more, and soon he felt a different spirit take hold of him. He drank what was left of his firewater. The kindly trader poured more. The spirit of the white man was with him. He was happy, happier than he had ever been! Now he and the trader were brothers. He regretted his selfish attitude towards the white trader—he must share his beaver pelts with his new friend. He put the magic gun back on the counter, untied the big bundle of pelts and pushed a pile towards the trader, who accepted and in return gave him more firewater. Dancing Light drank it in one gulp. He wanted more and more of the magic spirit of the white man that drove all his cares away. Eventually he gave his friend the remains of his huge bundle of furs and in return picked up two heavy crocks of firewater. On his way out he stopped at a large pile of oddly assorted clothing and put on a broadbrimmed hat with a plume, a sailor tunic with gold buttons, wagoner's trousers, and knee-high boots. The magic gun lay forgotten on the counter.

Gorgeously attired, he stepped outside. The first person he encountered was his opponent from the moccasin game. When he saw him, Dancing Light started to cry. He was ashamed of having deprived Scarface of all his pelts. He felt he should share his riches with the unfortunate man. Dancing Light offered Scarface some of the firewater. Scarface took a few swallows and soon he too started to cry. Great sobs convulsed their bodies. They embraced each other and together proceeded to Scarface's tent.

The tent was full of men, women and children. Happily Dancing Light shared his riches with everyone. He passed the crocks of firewater around. Soon they were all happy, singing and crying madly. Then two men started an argument over a woman. Enraged, one tried to hit the other with a club. He swung wildly and missed, hitting a child on the head instead. The mother of the child ran screaming from the tent. The occupants of the tent laughed uproariously at the man with the club, who, puzzled, looked at his club with astonishment. Some mocking remarks were made about his bad aim. Maddened with rage, the man plunged into the darkness after the fleeing woman. In a while an agonizing shriek was heard, but by that time the people in the tent had lost all interest in the affair and continued their carousing and drinking.

Dancing Light passed a crock of firewater to the friend who had brought him his luck. Great tears poured down his face—he had never been so happy! Scarface accepted the firewater and in return offered Dancing Light his wife. In the cramped tent the two started to dance. They discarded all their clothing but Dancing Light kept on his plumed hat. He put his arms around the woman and both of them lurched crazily from side to side. Suddenly, with a seductive leer on her face, she broke away from him and taunted him with her dance steps. With a terrible whoop, Dancing Light fell on her from behind, and as the woman chortled happily he pinned her down and took her. Afterwards they joined the rest of the party and with wild cries, and crazy laughter, finished what was left of the firewater. Finally they fell in a heap, one on top of the other, in a stupor.

Late the next day Dancing Light woke up from a nightmare with a dizzy head and a sick feeling in his belly. His mouth and nose were smarting and he realized the tent was full of smoke. He stumbled over the sprawled bodies of his drinking companions and Scarface's naked wife, only dimly aware of the previous night's happenings. Outside a storm was raging with flashes of lightning, and loud claps of thunder. In the distance he saw flames leaping towards the darkened sky. The trading post was burning! A crowd of frenzied Indians circled wildly round the fence. With war whoops and blood-curdling cries, they broke into the warehouse and gleefully scattered all the goods and the heavy kegs of firewater on to the field outside. The kegs were forced open and the cheering Indians helped themselves to the firewater.

No one paid any attention to the screams from inside the burning building. Without warning the trading post collapsed and the screams ceased. A mass of orange flames and bright cinders shot towards the sky.

At the height of the commotion Dancing Light spotted something on the ground. There was no mistaking it. Lying among the scattered barrels, spades, bales of calico, axes and saws, was the magic gun. He snatched it up and broke into a run. No one even looked at him. Soon the wild cries of the Indians were far behind and he was speeding in total darkness along the trail. He did not stop running until early morning when he reached his settlement.

Covered with soot and grime he entered Crooked Mouth's lodge. The hunter, hearing footsteps in his cabin, woke up with a start. Without a word Dancing Light handed him the magic gun. Crooked Mouth seized it greedily and, enraptured with this fantastic prize, did not notice as Dancing Light and the woman walked out.

In his lodge, Dancing Light sank exhausted to the ground. His wife kneeled beside him. Wearily he told her: "A lot of people would say there is an evil spirit in that place where the whites trade." But she, sensing that his mind was troubled, pulled him towards her bosom and let his head rest on her breast. With supple fingers she rubbed his wiry shoulders, neck and chest until all tension had left him. He was content at last. He would never trade her—not even for a barrelful of magic guns.

He moved closer. Deep inside her, he planted the seeds of Scarface's wife's disease.

Big Horn
Gives Birth
To a Calf

After the elderly members of the tribe had finished their respective tales, Paisk, a young and noble Indian, who often worked among the whites, addressed them.

"O Grandfathers of my people! I have listened to your stories with great respect. You have seen some wonderful things in your lifetime and have shown how powerful our medicine men were. But now that they are gone, we no longer have anyone to advise us, to cure us when we are sick, assist us in love, or to ward off evil spirits. Now we depend on the white people. But we are strangers to them—they do not understand our ways, and we do not understand theirs. So we frequently come to grief. If you would allow me I would like to tell you some stories of our time."

It happened not too long ago that Grandpa Big Horn felt sick. He had terrible pains in his belly. The old man was vigorous and had always been in good health, so he was not worried. He knew exactly what to do. He dosed himself with medicinal herbs and waited for the pains to go away. He belched a few times and passed gas. But nothing came of it. The pains became stronger, settled around his belly, and went to the back. Grandpa Big Horn was sick and miserable. He tossed and turned all night.

In the morning the pains were not any better, so he called his wife and told her to ask the doctor in town for help. Grandma Horn went to see the white doctor. She described Big Horn's trouble and implored the doctor to help her sick husband. The doctor listened to what she had to say and told her that before he could do anything for Big Horn he must have a bottle of his urine. Grandma left the doctor and went back to the reserve. She told Big Horn of the doctor's request for his urine.

The following morning Big Horn pissed into a bottle and told his young grandson to deliver it to town. The boy took it and started off towards the

town. On the way he saw a group of boys playing ball and having fun. The boy quickly forgot the old man's trouble. He put the bottle on the ground and joined the others in the game. Towards the end of the day, one of them fell and knocked over the bottle and the urine poured out on the ground. Dismayed, the boy picked up the empty bottle. He was still a long way from the town and did not know what to do. As he stood there, perturbed, he saw a cow standing in one corner of the field. Just as the animal raised its tail and started to piss, the boy picked up the empty bottle and soon had it filled with cow's urine. Then he ran all the way to town and left the bottle with the doctor.

Meanwhile Big Horn spent another miserable night. The pains were bad. "Never mind," he said, "tomorrow I'll have the medicine."

In the morning, the doctor came to see Big Horn, who was surrounded by his friends and relatives, all laughing and joking and trying to lift his spirits.

The white doctor looked at Big Horn, examined his tongue, held his wrist and poked his hand at Big Horn's belly. Then he got up and addressed the sick man: "Big Horn, I have some bad news for you. Mind you, your case is most unusual because you are not exactly sick, but you are not well either. In fact, you are pregnant. It grieves me to tell you that in some unaccountable manner you are about to give birth to a calf."

There was a horrified silence in the room. Not a word was spoken until the doctor went out. Once he had gone, Big Horn gave an agonized shriek that shook the walls.

"Oh my! How miserable and uncertain is my fate! That such a thing should happen to me! At my age. Indeed I must be punished for my own excesses and folly. Come to think of it, many times I did it in a most inappropriate and lazy manner! It must have leaked back and made me pregnant. And now that I am in this most unwelcomed state, how shall I go through this? I am not at all equipped for pregnancy. I have not got such a spacious and convenient hole for it to come out. Yes, my fate is most miserable. I used to live in this lodge in peace and once was respected by all my neighbours. Now my fate is most uncertain. What shall become of me? What will the people say? I see a lot of trouble ahead of me. The world's going to be a difficult place to live. I'll put my pants on, take my sack with some grub in it and leave you all."

In vain were the protestations of his wife, relatives and friends. Panting and grunting, feeling sick and ashamed of himself, Big Horn left his house on the reserve.

Very dispirited, he travelled aimlessly for many hours until he reached a large forest. Suddenly he stopped dead in his tracks. Bathed in the bright moonlight, swinging gently in the breeze there was the body of a man hanging from a tree! Around his neck he had a noose tied to one of the branches. Big Horn, although quite shaken by this unexpected encounter, moved a bit closer. The man was quite dead. His eyes were bulging out, and his face was swollen. It was then that Big Horn noticed the dead man's boots. They were the most beautiful pair of boots he ever saw. My! what beautiful boots! I would like to own them. He tried to pull them off but couldn't. The dead man's legs were too swollen. Big Horn pulled out his knife and cut the dead man's legs off and put the beautiful boots with the legs still inside them in his sack.

Big Horn continued on his way until he reached a farm. He knocked at the door, and the farmer and his wife welcomed him. Big Horn sat down, and just as the woman offered him some food, he was seized with great pains in his belly. He realized that his time was approaching very soon. The farmer noticed his distress and gave him a crock of whiskey. It tasted good. Big Horn had some more. In an hour there was no more whiskey in the crock. But there was no mistaking the great rumbling in his belly. "Well, here it comes," thought Big Horn, feeling very miserable. He was ashamed, however, to disgrace himself in front of the farmer and his wife. Hastily he made his excuses and rushed outside. There he passed much gas and started to defecate. He did this for a long time and afterwards, as he was quite drunk, he stumbled into the barn and collapsed on a pile of hay.

Early in the morning, he was awakened by the touch of something wet on his face. He opened his eyes and looked into the face of a young calf, licking his cheek. Big Horn looked at the calf in amazement. All at once he realized that he had no more pains in his belly. He, Big Horn, had given birth to this calf! Scared out of his wits, he jumped to his feet and ran off, leaving his sack behind.

Later that day the farmer went to inspect his barn. He saw the young calf licking the boots with the legs still inside. Great heavens! The calf must have devoured the poor Indian who came to visit them last night. He went home, fetched his gun and shot the man-eating calf.

Meanwhile Big Horn, greatly agitated after all of his exertions, told his wife: "You should have seen that calf I gave birth to, a monstrous and ferocious animal if ever there was one. It nearly ate me alive. I can't sleep with you any more! There's no telling what may happen if I get pregnant again!"

The men in the sweat lodge laughed at Big Horn's plight. He and his wife no longer pounded corn together and the farmer had shot his calf. None of this would have happened had Big Horn had the benefit of a sound medicine man.

The
Preacher

The men laughed heartily over Big Horn's misadventure. Then they were silenced by Paisk as he lifted his hand and again asked for their attention.

Not too many years ago, several Indian families lived by themselves in the bush. They rarely saw any white men, and as a rule kept their distance from these strangers. In one of the cabins there lived a comely Indian girl of gentle disposition. She kept very much to herself and seldom mixed with the others. The girl liked to walk in the woods where she had dreams and visions of faraway places quite unlike her crude surroundings. Somehow she knew that her life should be different, but she did not know what to do about it.

But then one day she heard an Indian from the south talk of the god and great spirit of the white man. He was a very powerful spirit who gave the white men strength and riches beyond all understanding. A long time ago, some bad people had caught this spirit and nailed him to a plank. Although he had suffered a great deal, he forgave them for what they had done. Soon afterwards he died and was brought down from the plank, but he tricked the people who had put him to death by coming to life again. Although he was invisible he could hear people around him quite clearly. When they wanted something from him they had to plead with him for a long time. He usually granted them their wishes, but first he liked to make them suffer to remind them of his suffering when he was nailed to that wooden plank.

Once she had heard of this great spirit the gentle Indian girl realized that this indeed was what she had been waiting for. She must communicate with him straight away. She learned that in the white man's town there was an enormous house in which there lived a man who talked every day with the great spirit. Her mind made up, she took her few possessions, said goodbye to her family and left for town.

65

She reached it after several hours, but then she became confused and quite lost. All the houses in the town were huge and she did not know where to go. But luck was with her. A kind old man directed her to the other side of town, and there indeed stood the largest house she had ever seen. Determined to find at once the man who knew the great spirit, she entered the big house. This happened to be the day on which people pleaded with the spirit and asked him for favours. In the huge room there were so many people that the Indian girl was barely able to find space for herself. The white people all held pieces of paper in their hands, and they were yelling and shouting together. In a much smaller room in front of the big one there stood an old man in a long white shirt and he too yelled.

The Indian girl was frightened by all the noise. She wondered what would happen if the great spirit became angry with the people. But then she realized that he was probably quite old by now, and perhaps his hearing was not what it used to be. The people had to shout at him in order to be heard. So the girl waited until the yelling stopped and all the people filed out of the room.

She stood there quite alone until the man in the long white shirt approached her. She explained the purpose of her visit. He was pleased.

"My child, you came here all by yourself to find him? Indeed his grace must be upon you as he brought you from the wilderness to this holy house."

And as it happened, the old preacher's housekeeper had left him and he was quite alone in the big house. So the girl became the new housekeeper. She cooked for the preacher, looked after his simple needs, and kept the big house clean. In return the preacher taught her the true ways of the spirit which made the white men superior to all other human beings.

Each evening, when her chores were done, she meditated and pondered on all the good works of the great spirit. At times she denied herself all food and water to suffer the way he had suffered for all wicked men. But what was her suffering compared to that of the spirit nailed alive to that plank?

One day the preacher, bent on some errand, entered the girl's room. He was amazed to see her lying naked on the cold stone floor with her arms outstretched. Startled, he turned to leave but, overcome by curiosity, he asked, "My child, what are you doing naked on that chilly floor?"

"It is my desire to suffer, to be cold and hungry," she replied. "In that way, I feel closer to him." She continued to gaze with rapture at the figure of the spirit nailed to the wooden plank above her door.

Meanwhile, the preacher had a good look at the girl lying fully exposed on the floor. As he stared at her he started to tremble and perspire, and at the same time experienced a very strange sensation under his cassock. Agitated, he gathered up his robe and rushed out of her room. It was not long, however, before he was back.

"My child," he said to her, "your devotion has surpassed my fondest hopes and expectations. Indeed you are his true follower. You have set me an

66

example, and it is only right that I too should follow. And if you are suffering on that cold chilly floor, then I shall suffer likewise." And with his heart pounding he took off his clothes and lay beside her on the floor.

In a while he began to moan and groan as if in pain. She turned towards him and was surprised to see a huge shaft stuck right in his lower belly. There was no mistaking his great distress.

"What is the matter?" cried the girl. "What is that pointed stick that stands out from your belly?"

"My child," he answered, "this stick is a thorn in my side, which causes me great pain and misery. Nevertheless, I have to endure it with fortitude and suffer the beastly thing. It is so firmly wedged inside me that I can't move it by myself."

And as he groaned and moaned on the cold floor the gentle Indian girl was unable to stand it any longer.

"It grieves me to see you so. Although I am cold and hungry, my suffering is but small compared to yours. And since you have followed me on to the cold floor, it is now my turn to follow you so that my tender flesh should suffer. I want you to torture me with that thorn of yours, and put it where it will hurt me most!"

She had hardly uttered these words when he was right on top of her and thrust his thorn in a most unexpected place. She groaned with pain as it sank deep inside her, but she resigned herself to it, and as the torture continued, she prepared herself to endure it. Suddenly, however, she experienced a most unusual sensation. Her body trembled and was convulsed by a great force which lifted her high up into the air until she reached the sky. All around her she saw celestial bodies and heard music. And as she floated high in space, the stars, which were bright and shiny, became red and orange and started to explode right inside of her. In a moment of great ecstasy she felt very close to the great spirit. After a while she came down from the sky and back to life. She rested quietly for a time beside the preacher, who still panted heavily after all the unaccustomed exercise.

After some thought she said, "It is only by suffering that we can be purged of all wickedness. Through suffering I have found his grace. I shall not abandon it easily but follow it with all my strength. Indeed there is no more time for me to cook or sew or to look after your big house. I must go out among my own people and suffer with them so that we may all attain a state of grace!"

The preacher was sorry to lose her. Nevertheless, afraid of what might happen if anyone found out how he had suffered with the girl, he reluctantly let her go.

Serene and happy, she travelled for quite a time until she reached the edge of the forest. There she built herself a small hut. One day a young Indian boy passed by and the girl invited him inside. To his surprise, the girl immediately stripped herself naked and lay down on the cabin floor with her arms outstretched. Before he could say a word the girl told him to lie down beside her. Puzzled, the Indian boy obeyed. Soon the boy started to moan, bothered by a large thorn. The Indian girl was pleased to see him suffer so.

"Now I will show you," she said to the feverish boy, "how through our suffering we can please the great spirit and he will give us grace as he gives it to white people. But since my flesh is not pierced by a big thorn like yours, you must make me suffer and share it with me too. So nail me to the floor with that big pointed stick in a place where it will hurt me most, and cause me as much pain as you please!" The boy, amazed by her pleas, the meaning of which he did not understand, only too willingly did as he was told. Three times he pierced her tender flesh with his thorn, and the girl suffered nobly and soon enough obtained the spirit's grace.

Afterwards, the Indian boy visited her little hut often. Eventually he told all his friends and cronies that there in the bush, quite alone, lived a gentle Indian girl who had to suffer on account of the great spirit of the white people. Word of this spread all around the Indian land, and the Indians flocked to her little cabin in the bush. They came from far and wide, from the villages and farms and forests. They came by canoe, on foot, and on horseback. They came singly and in large groups, old and young, fat and lean. And as they came they all took turns at the little shrine in the woods. They suffered with the girl and were purged of their wickedness. And to thank her for her saintly deeds, they brought her cigarettes and candy, and all kinds of trinkets.

One day an Indian who had drunk too much whiskey beat her in a fit of religious fervour. She was bruised and swollen and her lip was cracked wide open. The girl accepted it all with resignation. But a wily old Indian immediately sized up the situation. He built himself a shack nearby and kept a watchful eye on her. In return, he helped himself to most of her cigarettes and chewing gum, and from time to time, with her assistance, he too was purged of all his sins.

They lived like that for many years. One day a band of Indians from a far off land came to see her. But they found her hut empty, and she was never heard of again.

The
Lady
Teacher

The men in the sweat lodge laughed heartily at the story of the Indian girl who was deceived by the preacher. Indeed, some of them remembered her well. They too had attained grace through her.

Again Paisk spoke.

Not loo long ago and not too far from here there lived a young Indian woodsman. He was a simple man who lived by hunting birds and small game. In the fall he felled trees and cut them into logs which he sold on the reserve and in the town. He lived by himself in a small cabin in the bush and was content. He made no demands on anyone and was well liked by all.

One day during the fall the young woodsman arrived at the school in town. He had not been there since the year before, and was surprised to see a young woman at the schoolhouse. She was the new teacher. The Indian was completely overcome at the sight of her. He had never seen anyone so beautiful. The girl had deep blue eyes and long blonde hair which fell over her shoulders. She wore a white silk blouse with a ruffled front, and a short black pleated skirt. Her black shoes had very high heels which made her legs look very long. He stared at her, speechless.

The beautiful white teacher laughed at him. "Well, what do you want?" she asked.

He looked down so as not to show his embarrassment, and answered, "I have brought some wood for the school fire."

She smiled at him again. "Well, all right then, put it in the shed behind the school."

The woodsman went outside and laboured for quite a while. As he worked, the teacher watched him from the window. She noticed his lean and muscular body, his narrow sensitive face framed by long black hair, and the easy grace of his movements. His task completed, he came back. She offered him some tea.

"I have not seen you before," said the teacher.

"I am a free Indian," he replied. "I don't live on the reserve but in the bush in a cabin of my own." And being very shy in front of this lovely woman, and not knowing what to say to her, he took his leave abruptly and departed.

But he could not forget her. How beautiful she was, how different from the Indian girls he had known. He sat for many days in his cabin in the bush and brooded. "She must have put a spell on me. I can't get her out of my mind." Soon he ceased to work altogether.

One morning the woodsman heard some movement not far from his cabin and went outside to investigate. He was amazed to see the teacher alone and far away from the town. While he stood speechless not knowing what to say, the white woman greeted him in a friendly manner. She told him that she was collecting plants and flowers for her pupils. The woodsman, familiar with the forest, helped her and soon enough her satchel was overflowing with all kinds of plants, mushrooms and shrubs. Tired after her long walk and the oppressive heat of the day, she asked the woodsman if she could rest in his cabin for a while, and he invited her inside.

He lit a fire in the stove and made tea. They drank in silence, the white woman and the Indian man. But he could not help looking at her all the time. She, fully aware of his scrutiny, pretended not to notice. Her tea finished, she put the cup down and rose to leave. As she reached the door, there was a loud thunderclap. It was followed by another, and in no time there was a great wind pelting down rain and hailstones. This made her return to town quite impossible.

The Indian put more wood on the stove and made some fresh tea. When he handed her a cup their hands touched. He felt as if he had been scorched by fire. Both of them were breathing fast and, as they looked at each other, their eyes locked and they could not force themselves to turn away. She held her breath as he advanced towards her. He seized the submissive woman in his arms and carried her to his bunk. With great force he plunged into her, and as she received him she shuddered and cried out with pleasure. The Indian, in a great frenzy, pressed her to his body until he exploded. Covered with sweat he collapsed at her side.

Content and happy, they looked at each other tenderly. Before long, the sight of her aroused him once more and this time their passion surpassed the closed world of the tiny cabin. They completely lost themselves in each other, and their cries of pleasure merged with the storm that raged outside, until they and the storm were one.

Late at night, as the rain fell softly on the window panes, they woke up.

And once more the Indian was hard and erect like a club. This time she lowered her head and engulfed him with her mouth until his pleasure was so frantic that he nearly went out of his mind. With her soft manipulations she released the tension that was in him and with a sigh he passed out. Early next morning they left the cabin and walked to the outskirts of the town. There he left her.

The Indian, enamoured of the beautiful white woman, lived from one week to the next just waiting for her. The girl visited him when the white men had their days of prayer, and stayed with him until the following day. The woodsman worshipped her. She could drive him into the wildest frenzy with her gentle manipulations. And the white woman herself was happy to please him.

They went on like that for quite a while. But when winter came the teacher could no longer visit the cabin of her lover. The Indian people were surprised when the young woodsman abandoned his cabin in the bush and moved in with a family on the reserve, but they did not ask any questions. From the reserve it was not too far to town and the Indian hoped to visit his beloved at the school. However, his numerous requests to meet her there were all in vain.

"I have taken enough risks already," she told him. "I cannot possibly see you at the school. We will wait until springtime and then I will visit you again." She was very firm, and the poor woodsman became more and more frustrated as the time went on.

To make matters worse he had not worked since he had met her and now he had no food or money. Eventually he got a card from the white boss on the reserve, and with it he obtained food in town. After a while he got into the habit of selling his food back to the grocer and with this money he bought beer. Soon he found out that when he was drunk he could forget the beautiful woman in town. And while drunk he tried to tell the Indian girls how he and the white woman had loved and been happy. But the Indian girls were too shy to please him in that way and when he began to beat and abuse them, they stopped seeing him altogether.

One day, drunk and crazed with desire, he knocked at the teacher's door. At first she did not recognize the dirty, wasted Indian who reeked of stale beer. But as he spoke to her and tried to explain the purpose of his visit she recognized her former lover and screamed with horror. Soon a crowd of white people surrounded him, beat him up, and threw him in jail.

Many months later he returned to the reserve. An old woman who had no chance of getting a man of her own got hold of him and he stayed with her. When he was drunk, which was very often, he tried to explain to the old woman how he and the beautiful white woman had loved each other. The old woman tried to please him, but it was in vain. How could she possibly have satisfied him, an old woman who was not trained in the arts and who had never had any schooling?

The young Indian drank more and more and died well before his time. He was buried by the old woman who had looked after him. Afterwards, the old woman often discussed him with her cronies. They shook their heads and never ceased to wonder what it was all about.

The
Evil
Spell

The men had listened attentively as Paisk told them the story of the woodsman who had come to grief because of a white woman. They felt sorry for him and their hearts were troubled.

Whispering Dawn, a tall brave with a light complexion, stood to speak. For a long time Whispering Dawn had lived in the big city among the whites and he knew them very well. At one time he had been married to a white woman. However, he did not like life among the whites and had settled among the Indians just outside the reserve. He told them his story.

Only a few years ago on a nearby reserve, an elderly Indian couple lived in comfort and contentment. They had several children, all of them grown up and married, except their youngest daughter, Rosana. Although still very young, the girl was amply endowed with womanly charms, and in spite of her tender years, she was not inexperienced in life. Whenever she was alone in the woods or berry-picking in the bush, several Indian boys would follow her. After several arguments and quarrels, one of them would stay behind with the girl, and she rarely got home before dark. At times these quarrels got out of hand and the boys would fight for her and this, of course, gave Rosana a tremendous thrill. It was fun to be young and desirable.

She lived in this happy and carefree manner for a number of years. Eventually the news of what was happening reached the ears of the white preacher in town. He called on her parents, both devout Christians, and threatened them with hell and damnation because of their wanton daughter. He lectured them for a long time, and when they were properly cowed he addressed the old man.

"And you!" he cried, "think of your position, the janitor in the white man's school. How can you allow this wickedness to continue? Marry her to a good Christian, and marry her soon!" In the end the old couple promised to obey his wishes.

At home they confronted their high-spirited daughter and informed her of the preacher's warning. But although the girl did not object to marriage, her choice was limited—in fact it was very difficult. She knew all the available men in the village, most of them intimately. Some of them pleased her when she was berry-picking, but none of them pleased her for long. Why pick berries from one bush when there were so many? She remained in this state of indecision for quite a time while still continuing in her free ways, to the great concern of her people and the stern disapproval of the preacher. Although the old couple never reproached her openly or asked her to change her ways, their silent accusations disturbed her and took some of the joy from her otherwise happy and gay disposition.

The news of the meeting between Rosana's parents and the preacher did not remain unreported on the reserve for long. Soon all the tongues in the village were wagging, and some enterprising individuals even laid bets on one or two of the more promising young men.

One day as the old man was returning home from the white man's town, he was accosted by Black Sam. Sam was a quiet man who never caused any trouble, and yet people found him quite mysterious. He lived alone and kept very much to himself. His hair was already grey, but he was still tough and wiry, and he walked like a young man. What bothered the Indians, however, were Black Sam's eyes. They were dark and smouldering, and when Sam looked at people, his stare chilled the very marrow of their bones. Disconcerted, they could not return his stare for long and had to look away. Because of his strange black eyes and general aloofness, people tried to avoid him whenever possible.

So Rosana's father was startled by this unexpected encounter. His anxiety increased when Sam said to him, "I hear that Rosana is to marry, and I quite agree that she should have a man. However, before you go any further with your plans, I feel that it's only right that I should inform you of my intentions. I live alone and there is no one to look after my needs. Rosana will suit me well. I want her as my woman. I think my request is not at all unreasonable. I'll look after her well."

The old Indian, unable to look the man in the face, stuttered in reply, "Why, you can't! In fact it's quite impossible. How can you speak like that of my youngest daughter, you who are not even a Christian? You are even older than I am. No, I can't possibly allow it."

Agitated, the old man left Sam and hurried home to tell his wife of their conversation. She shook her head in disbelief, and agreed with her husband that they could not possibly let Rosana live with Black Sam. But the old couple were uneasy. They were afraid of the harm he might do to them if he were seriously offended, and because of that they hoped to avoid him altogether.

News in a small settlement has a way of travelling. In no time it spread all around the village and soon reached the ears of the preacher. Again he called on the old couple.

"Black Sam? That old man? A pagan, heathen anti-Christ! I forbid it! Your tender child must not be taken by that beastly man. Marry her to a decent Christian!" Faced with his wrath the perplexed old couple promised to find a suitable man for their daughter and to marry her off as soon as possible.

The following day on his way to the school, Rosana's father was again confronted by Black Sam. This time Black Sam did not say anything—he merely looked at the old man and fixed him with his horrible eyes, until the old man dropped his head and stared uneasily at his feet. His legs felt heavy and his body numb. He desperately wanted to get away, but the spell held him there and kept his legs firmly rooted to the ground. After what seemed a very long time, he collected his senses and looked around. He found himself alone. There was no sign of Black Sam. Deeply troubled, he continued his journey to town.

Once more their encounter was noticed, and in a few hours it had become common knowledge on the reserve, and his wife had heard of it as well.

The old man still felt Black Sam's terrible gaze drilling right through his skull. It filled his mind with dreadful forebodings and he found his chores at the school unusually hard. And because his thoughts were elsewhere, he slipped and fell, rolling down the staircase right to the bottom. His legs were broken. The doctor set them in plaster casts and told him that he would never walk again. He was sent home in a wagon.

News of this dreadful accident soon spread around the reserve. There was fear on many faces and people kept their distance from Black Sam. The old Indian's wife, usually docile, was stunned by the disaster and confronted her unruly daughter.

"It's time you listened to your elders!" she cried. "Because you continued in your selfish ways, you exposed us all to grievous harm. Now you'll obey my wishes. I'm taking you to Black Sam!"

The daughter, bewildered by this unexpected decision, hesitated, but her mother slapped her hard across the face and grabbed her by the arm. She dragged the reluctant girl past a group of people gathered outside the house, who, although curious, pretended not to notice when the old lady, the girl trailing behind her, entered Black Sam's house.

Black Sam seemed quite unconcerned with the unusual visit. It seemed as if he had been expecting them to come. The old lady pushed Rosana towards him and cried, "You wanted her and she's yours, but harm us no more!" And before he could answer, she slammed the door and was gone.

Rosana was frightened now that she was alone with him, but somehow all thoughts of running away left her. Speechless, she stared numbly at the floor, her head bowed. Old Sam came towards her and looked at her kindly. When he commanded her to undress and pointed out his cot near the stove, she obediently dropped her dress to the floor and lay on the cot. He sat beside her, and as his hand travelled gently over her silky hair, firm young breasts and belly, some of the fear left her and she gave him a warm smile. He continued his caresses and when his hand rode lightly under the smooth swell of her stomach, she gasped, held her breath and sighed deeply. Then he undressed and she looked at him in surprise. His purple-veined penis stood solid, erect, and hard. She reached out for him but he was much too big for her hand to grasp. Soon she was in his arms and he was crushing her beneath his weight. But he did not hurry and in a little while Rosana found herself transported beyond her wildest dreams.

Afterwards Rosana rested happily by his side. Never before had she experienced such great contentment. No longer afraid, she caressed him gently until he, aroused, covered her again with such force that she begged for mercy.

And so Rosana stayed with Black Sam. Part of it was her fear of that dark man who had such power in his eyes, and who had obviously wanted her. It drove away all foolish thoughts from her head. He never tried to humour or particularly please her, but in his own way he treated her with kindness. It often happened that, while she busied herself with her chores, she would be startled by his stare. It made her feel weak and shaky, and then moist and feverish with desire. Rosana knew what he wanted and would drop whatever she was doing and go to him. She was always willing to comply with his wishes which were really very much like her own.

In a short time she became grateful for the unexpected turn of events which had brought her to Black Sam. The women in the village treated her with respect, and were, in fact, envious of the comely girl who had now assumed a position of importance amongst them.

In vain the preacher stormed and threatened from his pulpit. She was happy with Sam. The old lady, afraid of the preacher, ceased to attend his services, and once the plaster was off, the old man started to walk without crutches. And the people nodded their heads and interpreted it as another sign of Black Sam's power. They thought that he was no longer angry at Rosana's father; the girl was his and he removed his evil spell.

In due course, Rosana gave birth to a baby. However, as she spent most of her time with Sam who wanted her all to himself, her parents took care of the child. One day, the old couple were visited by the preacher. He admired Rosana's baby, but he did not fail to remind them that the innocent young child, born out of wedlock, would go to hell if it were not baptised. Once more the old couple were disturbed and at a loss to know what to do. This time the preacher would not give up. He visited them often and urged them to save the poor baby's soul. If they hesitated he pressed them harder until eventually they yielded to his wishes. The baby was taken to town and baptised by the preacher. To their relief Black Sam did not seem to mind; he merely laughed and Rosana made fun of them too.

A month later the baby developed a chest condition with a cough and a fever. In spite of all the doctor's efforts, it died.

If they felt any sorrow, Rosana and Sam did not show it; they accepted it quietly and spoke of the baby no more. More than ever Rosana gave Sam her warmest affection, and he continued to treat her in his firm but gentle manner. Because of this she was envied by the other women, and this envy must have turned the fates against them. Rosana arrived home one day to find Sam speechless and in a wild condition. Before she had time to find the doctor Sam had suffered a stroke and died.

Utterly crushed, Rosana spent a lonely winter, rarely going outside her house. She brooded, and often her thoughts turned to Sam. But then spring arrived and with it a restlessness and a feeling that life was passing her by. Her gay and happy disposition reasserted itself. Alone in her house, she felt very much in need of company, and reasoned that it was only right for one so young.

One warm spring day two Indian boys went visiting in the village. They carried with them a crock of home-brew which they tasted freely until they felt quite light-headed and in need of an amorous adventure. They visited several Indian homes and shared their home-brew with a number of people. However, they were not too well received by the objects of their attention. Undismayed, they returned home, refilled their crocks, and again started out on their search for congenial and obliging females. They tried for several hours but had no luck. Around midnight they found themselves in front of Black Sam's house. They knew that Rosana, so young and beautiful, lived there all by herself. But the memory of that terrible old man with the evil eyes who had once possessed her made them hesitate. Eventually, one of them, a braggart and a bully who was by now fairly intoxicated, screwed up enough courage and decided to walk in. With the crock under his arm he entered the house and found Rosana asleep in the kitchen. Although startled by the noise Rosana recognized the caller. She had known him well many years ago when she had first gone berry-picking in the bush.

When he offered her the brew, she accepted, taking a few mighty swallows. It tasted awful and sent shivers down her spine, but in a short time the brew gave her a warm and pleasant feeling. She felt relaxed, gay, and drank some more. Before long she was giddy. Rosana looked at the Indian boy and found him quite attractive. She gave him a warm and happy smile. And he, encouraged by the vast amount of brew he had consumed and that smile, lay down beside her and pulled her close. He ripped open her night-shirt, and with her soft warm body in his arms, did not waste any time.

Afterwards, quite drunk, he rolled off her and soon started to snore.

Rosana awoke early next morning. Her mouth was dry and she had an awful headache. Her nightshirt was torn to pieces and the crock lay shattered on the floor. The young Indian still slept beside her. In spite of her wretched condition, she accepted the situation; it was better than being so utterly lonely.

The young man began to visit Rosana often, and invariably brought some home-brew along with him. The girl developed quite a taste for the sweet-sour drink. When she had drunk enough she found that she did not even mind his frequent beatings. He kept Rosana a virtual prisoner in her house. Insanely jealous, he would not let her look at another man. But he was respected and envied by all his cronies in the village as the sole possessor of the beautiful girl.

However, he got more than he expected. One day he was summoned to the preacher and received a thorough tongue-lashing.

"If you want her then you must marry her!" cried the preacher. "But you must stop this dissolute behaviour, for if you don't, then the devil will take you and you will burn in hell like Black Sam!" The sullen boy, who was a coward and only found his courage in alcohol, gave in to the persistent preacher and agreed to marry Rosana.

They had a large church wedding, and Rosana, fortified by liquor, looked almost happy in spite of her one black eye. The boy, who felt that he had been trapped into marriage, was mean and resentful. But his disposition improved when, during the tremendous feast, his cronies made a fuss of him and his photo was taken with the beaming preacher. Afterwards he became completely drunk and remembered very little of the wedding.

As time went on, his resentment towards the girl increased. Now that he was married to her she was no longer admired by his friends. To make matters worse, Rosana was expecting a baby and was not so attractive anymore. So he drank more and more and complained against his fate. He flew into terrible rages and often beat her. One day he kicked her in the stomach and as a result the baby died. Rosana no longer felt that need which made her crave a man. Most of the time she was scared and lonely. No longer was she the happy girl of old. Their envy long since forgotten, the women on the reserve felt sorry for her and pitied the unhappy creature. This, of course, only incensed her husband even more.

At last, in desperation, Rosana took the advice of an old lady and went to town to ask the preacher who had married her if it would be possible to unmarry. She had to leave that cruel husband who made her life intolerable. But the preacher, shocked at this proposal, sternly reminded her of her marriage obligations. She must be gentle and kind to her husband and forget her foolish ideas. Her protests fell on deaf ears and she was sent back to the reserve.

It did not take long for her husband to find out about Rosana's visit to the preacher and he was infuriated. He knew, quite rightly, that it had discredited him with the Indian people. That evening, in a drunken frenzy, he tried to kill Rosana, but as he was choking her, she grabbed a kitchen knife and stabbed him through the belly.

Rosana was charged with murder and was taken to the white man's town for trial. There the white boss from the reserve, who had some knowledge of the case, spoke up for her, and she was acquitted. Rosana returned to the village, but did not go back to her house, so full of unhappy memories. Instead she stayed with her parents where she spent a long and miserable winter. With spring, her anxiety departed and her good humour returned. Still young, she regained much of her lost beauty and she often walked by herself in the woods. By late summer she was in full bloom. Once more she went berry-picking in the bush, and more often than not, she was followed by a man. She gave her favours freely. One day she would find the right man. But even with no one around she really did not mind. Alone in the woods, Rosana was free and happy, and was loved all the time by the soft rain, the fresh wind, and the bright warm sun.

The Indian
and the
Tall Fair Lady

The men sat in silence pondering Whispering Dawn's story. Paisk interrupted their thoughts with another tale.

Not long ago, the white people of this land had a big celebration which they called the centennial of Canada. For this celebration they invited many people from strange and faraway places. The Indians were also invited to join the celebration and were asked to build their wigwam on an island in the river opposite the big city that was the meeting place for all the people. The Indians who had lived in this land for thousands of years were surprised by this celebration, but so as not to offend their white brothers, they agreed to the proposal.

They came from the four corners of the land to the big city and to the island in the river where their wigwam stood. With paint brushes, chisels, hammers and saws, they set out to make their wigwam something special.

But they were surprised when, in spite of all the enormous buildings in the city, there was nowhere for them to stay. "All filled up," they were told, "you'll have to try elsewhere." So the Indians had to find accommodation among their own people on the reserves outside the city.

But there was one man who had better luck than the rest. He was a tall, young Indian with laughing eyes and a dark merry face. In knee-high cowboy boots, tight white denim trousers, and a fringed leather jerkin, he was a fine figure of a man. But his head was always in the clouds; it was filled with dreams and because of these he frequently came to grief. He arrived in the city full of hope. As a representative of the Indian people, he fully expected to command the respect and admiration of the people in the city. They would point him out on the street, and some of them, more daring than the rest, would ask him questions about the fine Indian wigwam on the island in the

river. Patiently he would explain it all to them. But his most cherished dream was that of a lovely fair lady who, somewhere in this enormous city, was waiting for him. He imagined that she would introduce him to all the important people and she would show him the splendour of that magic city. Afterwards, when the two of them were alone, they would love each other. He would marry her and stay forever in that enchanted land.

Such were his dreams. For the moment, however, no one took any notice of him or cared enough to give him a place to stay. All day he tried to find a room, but no one wanted him. By the time it got dark he had given up all hope of ever finding a bed of his own. The tall buildings and the crowds of madly rushing people made him miserable and depressed. He had walked for hours along never-ending streets when he came across a dingy brick building. Above the door was a blue neon sign which read "The Paradise." The Indian pressed the bell and the door opened by itself.

"Come on up," a voice shouted from above. He ascended the narrow, dimly lit staircase, and on the first landing he found himself in a kitchen. There sat a dumpy old lady who said, "We're not ready yet!"

But the Indian implored her: "You don't understand. I come from a faraway northern land. I work at the wigwam on the island in the river; I have no place to spend the night!"

The old lady listened. "Well, I don't know," she said, "this is a very busy place but I've one small room right at the top of the stairs. It has a bed—you can have a look."

She led the Indian to a dark room in the attic. It had one tiny window covered with soot and grime. The plaster on the ceiling was falling off in great chunks and one bare electric bulb dangled over the bed. There was no room to walk around the bed and cockroaches swarmed in all directions, angry at this invasion of their domain.

But the Indian was only too happy to find a place of his own. He gratefully accepted the old lady's offer and made that dingy little room his home. In time he became quite friendly with his landlady. He entertained her with stories of his people, and, as he had quite a sense of humour, told some Indian jokes which made the old lady collapse in fits of laughter. She came to like the Indian and treated him well. Invariably she had a large supper ready for him after work and in the warm and cosy kitchen of "The Paradise" they talked and joked for hours.

The Indian was quite happy but one thing disturbed him: he found it difficult to get any sleep. Although the people in the city worked hard all day, at night there was no such thing as sleep. "The Paradise," forlorn and deserted during the day, was transformed at night into a place of gay parties, loud music and wild dancing. All sorts of games were played: Blind Man's Bluff, games of chance, and one in particular—racing up and down the stairs. The loser had to disrobe completely and if a man to provide some booze.

The
Squaw
Man

The men listened to Paisk's story with great interest, and indeed some of them remembered well that island in the river where the Indians had been asked to celebrate with the whites.

Within the sacred sweat lodge they would make no comment on the way the whites treated them, but they understood it only too well. Time and again the whites meddled in the affairs of the Indians, even when they were not asked for advice. At every opportunity they paid lip service to freedom, and yet they did not give it to the Indians.

Whispering Dawn raised his voice and told them the story of the white boss of the reserve.

This white boss had the largest house on the reserve. In front stood a tall pole with a flag to show the Indians that they were respected citizens of Canada with rights equal to all. The boss lived in the spacious house with his yellow-haired wife. The house itself was equipped with all kinds of comforts that the Indians on the reserve had not seen before. His wife did not have to chop wood, scrub floors, or do any heavy chores, since she had machines to do it all for her. These machines cooked her meals, washed her dishes and the clothes, and kept the big house warm and bright. The Indians did not envy her these riches, but they would have been proud to have such a lady as a friend, and to have their shy but friendly overtures accepted. This, however, was not the case. She treated them all with scorn, and made it clear that, as far as she was concerned, the Indians did not exist. In fact, she really hated the Indians. She, who did no work at all, never ceased complaining to her friends in town of how much she resented living among these savages who were so dirty and lazy.

As time went on her complaints increased. She blamed it all on her husband and it was not entirely without reason. At first her husband was made welcome in the white man's town. On Sundays, after church, while his wife gossiped with her friends, he would enjoy a game of cards with the policeman, the grocer, and the tavern-keeper.

One day he was surprised to learn that the Indians, in need of ready cash, had pledged their welfare cheques to the grocer months ahead of time. For this they received about half of the cheques' value in cash. The Indians knew quite well that they were getting the worst of the exchange, but they had learned long ago not to argue with the grocer and to accept what was given them. Quite often the money was spent on beer at the tavern. Beer was dispensed freely as long as the Indians could pay for it. A little beer travelled fast on an empty stomach, and it did not take long for the shy Indians to become happy and gay. And the policeman, who really had little work to justify his existence, waited eagerly for this to happen. As soon as the boisterous, happy Indians stepped outside the tavern, he clamped them all in jail. In the morning they were fined by the grocer, who was also the justice of the peace.

The boss was quite blunt with his friend the grocer. He told him plainly that from now on this exchange must cease, and if it did not, the grocer would be in deep trouble. This warning upset the grocer, as he realized he would not be able to trade with the Indians to his advantage. The tavern-keeper was also upset as there were only a few Indians with cash to spend in the tavern. And the policeman, deprived of his fun, was furious. There were no longer any Indians to put in jail and the townspeople were unimpressed with his position. After a while, the preacher also became annoyed with the boss, when he told the Indians that they, like the whites, could play and fish and have fun on Sundays. The number of Indians at the preacher's Sunday services dwindled, and the collection plate weighed considerably less. So, all in all, the white people, although they pretended to have nothing to do with the Indians, nevertheless depended on them a great deal and certainly did not object to their money. They still did well for themselves, but, deprived of their little extras, they were angry with the boss on the reserve, and waited for an opportunity to get even.

The boss, however, seemed quite unconcerned with what they thought of him. His days were busy since he had many Indians to look after, and each day he had to tackle large stacks of paper from his superiors in the city. There were endless forms to fill in and often he worked well into the night on the white, yellow, and green papers, and on his monthly, quarterly and annual reports.

The Indians were puzzled to see their boss constantly occupied with so much paper. They teased him about it and tried to get him to visit them instead.

"There are lots of fish in the Indian Lake," they told him. "We will have a feast and afterwards we'll sing and dance and be happy. And don't forget to bring along some of your paper; it will be useful to start the fire!"

The white man realized that there was some truth in what the Indians were saying; the endless forms nearly drove him to distraction. On top of all this, he was lonely; he had no friends to turn to, and the woman he had married was selfish and concerned only with what was good for herself. He sighed and went on with his paperwork.

Meanwhile, unknown to him, the great master of life had set in motion a series of events which was to steer his life in a most unexpected direction. One day, as he was walking towards the reserve, he felt a gentle breeze and with it there came an awful smell from the direction of the Indian Lake. The boss hurried to investigate, and as he ran towards the lake, he was joined by Indians who were also puzzled by the unusual smell. When they arrived at the lake they found it covered with dead fish. The whole lake was a stinking, rotting mess. The Indians were speechless as they surveyed the disaster, for they depended on the fish from that lake for their living. They were completely at a loss and did not know what to do.

The boss walked all around the lake until he came to a fast-flowing stream running into it. As usual it was bubbling noisily over the rocks, but now the water was no longer clear. It was full of a foamy, slimy, greenish liquid. The boss ran along its course to investigate and found that it was the same all the way. Eventually he arrived at a large brick building which he had never seen before. It was a chemical plant—the first one in the area of the white man's town. Naturally the citizens were proud to have such a modern industry near their town since it provided them with extra jobs and money.

The boss stormed inside, confronted the owner of the building, and told him what had happened to the fish in the lake. The owner of the building only laughed, and exclaimed impatiently: "You must be joking! We are busy here so you'd better leave, and don't bother us with dead fish!" The boss stormed out of the building, determined to do something to clean up the lake.

He appealed for help from people in the town but they too laughed at him and said he was mad. So he wrote and phoned his superiors in the city until the owner of the chemical plant was forced to give in and pay for a clean-up of the plant's waste. The owner was mad at the grocer who had sold him the land near the stream, and they were all furious with the boss of the reserve who had brought them nothing but trouble.

The boss was relieved when he saw that the slimy green liquid no longer dirtied the lake. However, the Indians had lost their fish and some of them went hungry. Again he wrote to his superiors, but this time they did not reply. He was, in fact, surprised when his bosses sent him fewer and fewer forms, and no directives at all to carry out.

Meanwhile, his wife, who never ceased to scold him for his stupidity, had decided to visit her mother in the city. She stayed week after week until finally she wrote saying that she did not wish to see him again. Her absence was soon noticed in town and people shook their heads. They were not sorry for her husband; obviously he did not deserve better.

The boss was utterly lost in the empty house, and he found the sudden lack of work very puzzling. Now he had lots of time to think of his wife who had left him, and he felt sorry for her once he realized that even in the city she would never be happy. Nevertheless he was very lonely; he had no friends and he longed for the company of a woman. He was attracted to the lady teacher in town, but she did not encourage his attentions. He was still a married man and he understood her reservations. Once he spotted the lady teacher by herself in the woods. He wanted to join her but she seemed so preoccupied that he followed her instead. He saw her enter the cabin of the woodsman where she remained long after darkness fell. The boss kept her secret to himself.

With very little work to do he was free to roam the countryside around the reserve. He used to walk in the woods and, one day, deep in the forest, he discovered a clear blue lake which was full of fish. He visited the spot many times thereafter. Propped against a large rock he puffed contentedly on his pipe and enjoyed the peace which surrounded him. At times he did a bit of fishing but more often than not he just sat there and did absolutely nothing.

One afternoon, as he rested beside the lake, he was startled by the sound of footsteps near him.

Turning around he saw a slender Indian girl, and as he emerged from behind the rock, the girl stopped dead in her tracks, frightened. She was still hesitating when he beckoned her towards him. She overcame her shyness and sat beside the tall white man. He questioned her gently and she told him that she often bathed in this lake. Her people lived outside the reserve, although they still fished and trapped and worked in the bush. While she talked the boss busied himself with his pipe, but from time to time he stole a glance at her. She appealed to him. He liked her softness and grace, her shy smile, and the way she tried, without success, to keep her long unruly hair in place. And she, in turn, looked in awe at the white man who was the boss of the reserve. The white man and the Indian girl felt at ease with each other, and yet, they dared not admit this even to themselves. It was only a casual encounter and towards the end of the day they parted company.

In the week that followed the boss again visited the blue lake. He took his fishing equipment with him, but fishing was not really on his mind. He was more than glad when he heard the soft footsteps behind him, and he saw the lovely Indian girl. She, too, was happy to see him. For a whole week she had not stopped thinking of him, and at night had found it difficult to sleep. There was no mistaking their mutual attraction as they greeted each

other. Their language was that of the eyes and of subtle tender gestures. They spent many happy and contented hours beside the blue lake deep in the thick forest, and the boss realized that he was no longer lonely. He began visiting the lake more frequently, and more often than not, the Indian girl was there waiting for him.

One evening as they rested beside a cheerful fire they heard someone approaching and looked up to see the lady teacher from town. The boss was happy to see her and asked her to join them but she excused herself and hurried back to town.

The following day, in an off-hand manner and not meaning any harm, she said to the principal of her school, "You'll never guess it! Last night I saw the administrator of the reserve with a lovely Indian girl." The same evening the principal told his wife what he had heard from the teacher. And she, like most frustrated people, was ready to assume the worst in others. She rushed off to the grocer's wife with the news: "The administrator was seen out in the bush with a young Indian girl. I don't have to tell you the rest," she concluded with a leer.

Soon it was on everybody's lips that the boss from the reserve cohabited with an Indian girl. There were even some who volunteered the information that they had seen him with many different Indian girls. They were indignant that he would take advantage of his high position to fool around with these ignorant Indians. He no doubt seduced these young women and forced them to commit unspeakable depravities. No wonder then that many of them ended up on the streets of the city. And what kind of example was his debauchery to the Indian men on the reserve?

At this time a solitary Indian happened to annoy the tavern-keeper, who, along with some infuriated whites, beat him up. Bruised and sore, the Indian ran back to the reserve and warned the others that the whites were up to no good. The Indians, sensing trouble, prudently decided to stay away from the town. Their absence was soon noticed by the white people, and this confirmed their worst suspicions. The thought of the Indians running wild inflamed the imaginations of the whites. They began heaping accusations on the boss of the reserve, and on the hapless Indians. No white woman was allowed alone outside the village. The policemen organized patrols of vigilantes to keep them under constant protection.

On Sunday, the preacher addressed his sermon to the "nobility of the White Man." "There are some," he thundered, "who are worse than the savages; the savages don't know any better. But the administrator? He has no excuses! He has no remorse for his hideous sins! We must weed him out like a poisonous plant." And as he thundered on, the congregation nodded their heads in righteous indignation.

They drew up a petition, signed by all the citizens of the town, and sent it to the big city. Their accusations struck a responsive cord with the administrator's superiors. For a long time they had found the boss of the reserve too much of a nuisance for their own comfort. He constantly made demands for his Indians. When they did not comply with his demands, he became quite objectionable and caused trouble.

A few days later the boss received an official letter from his superiors in the city. They told him to relinquish his position at the reserve, and return to the city. The boss, stunned by the letter, appealed to his superiors, but they refused to listen and dismissed him.

Soon the news of his imminent departure spread all around the reserve and also to the white man's town. The Indians were sorry to lose the man they had learned to trust. The townspeople were jubilant.

The man, who was a boss no longer, packed his belongings, said goodbye to the Indians, and prepared to leave. But he could not go without first seeing his beloved, and so made his way to the lake. His heart leapt with joy when he saw her. They greeted each other with great tenderness, talked of little things, and afterwards, as both of them were sad, they started a fire. On red hot stones they cooked fresh lake trout and heated water for their tea.

But it was left untouched. For, after a while, he said to the Indian girl, "You know I have to leave this place very soon. It was all very unexpected, and now there is very little that I can do here."

The Indian girl stared intently at the fire and replied very softly, "I know, I know, and yet I wish it were not true."

Encouraged by her reply, he told her as calmly as he could, "I would like to take you with me, but I can't do that. I am a married man, and I need a legal paper to set me free so that I can marry you . . . " Embarrassed, and unable to express his feelings, he stopped.

He was totally disconcerted when the girl started to laugh; in fact she seemed quite happy in spite of his obvious misery. Gently she turned towards him and said: "If you want my opinion, I must say that for a big white man, the boss of my people, your talk is foolish and hard to under-stand. You see, I am an Indian and I don't need any white man's paper to tell me when I am free or when to love a man. If you want me as much as I want you, why, you may as well have me right now. I will follow you gladly wherever you go."

He was stunned with her reply. With her invitation he stiffened and grew hungry with desire for her. He wanted to put his arms around her slender waist and melt her entire body into his. But he restrained himself and in a hoarse voice said, "Please wait for me until I get my freedom. I'll be back by springtime, or sooner if I can. Then I will marry you." The girl looked at him curiously as he hurriedly got to his feet and left.

The white man rushed off to the city in search of the paper to set him free. But he did not see her in the spring, since the official paper was hard to get and cost a great deal of money. Summer came and went and it was not until early winter that, armed with the legal decree, he rushed back to claim his Indian bride. But he was told that she had gone to the north country and no one had heard of her since. In desperation he searched the length and breadth of the Indian country, but all in vain. Bitterly he regretted his folly and the accursed official paper. In a rage he threw it away.

Lonely, miserable, and with no money, he went back to the blue lake. There the friendly Indians helped him to build a small cabin on the edge of the lake. There he leads a simple life, does a bit of fishing and hunting, and enjoys his solitude. But most of the time he is patiently waiting. He knows for certain that one day he will hear her soft footsteps near him and that this time he will never let her go.

That confused white man, who would not accept life as it was, and who gave up happiness for a piece of paper, exists no more. Only Whispering Dawn waits for his beloved, certain that one day she will surely come.

The
Dispossessed

Whispering Dawn finished the story of his own life and lapsed into silence. The Indians stirred themselves in the cramped interior of the sweat lodge and looked affectionately at the tall white man whose fate had brought him there. He had accepted the name they gave him, adopted their simple ways, and had, in fact, become an Indian. Frequently he went away on journeys and they did not see him for long periods. But then, unexpectedly, he would reappear and the Indians, always happy to have him back, would gather round, and with their good-natured merriment and laughter try to cheer him up.

Now there were no more stories to be told in the darkness of the sweat lodge. The charred stones had cooled. For the last time the Indians prostrated themselves on the cedar floor and gave their thanks to the spirit of the lodge. Then the door was thrown open and they went out into the dawn.

Naked, they ran down to the bank of the stream and plunged into the icy waters. Cleansed of dust and smoke, they scrambled back to the shore where they stood erect like statues and faced the sun as it slowly ascended on the horizon. Silently they offered their thanks to the morning sun, the new sweet earth and the great spirit which was all around them.

They ran back to the sweat lodge and built a fire from its birch saplings and cedar boughs. They gathered round it and as the flames leapt and darted towards the clear sky, they clapped their hands, stamped their feet, and chanted sacred prayers. Once the fire was gone, they scattered the charred, blackened stones all over the grassy field. Now nothing remained of the sweat lodge but a darkened hollow.

The sun was high when the Indians dressed again. In their denims, checkered shirts and brightly coloured scarves, they started back to the reserve. The younger ones shouldered the packs and the old men picked up their heavy canes. A few decided they wanted tobacco, so they headed for town instead.

They were an odd group, young and old, dressed in cheap, faded clothing. But they felt at peace. The spirit of the sweat lodge and a feeling of a common brotherhood was with them all. Under the sunny sky they ambled contentedly across the grassy meadow, the deep ravine and through the bush. A wooden fence marked the end of the trail, and also of the reserve; on the other side lay the rich brown fields of the white man's land. They stopped there for a while, watching a hawk circle lazily high up in the sky. Their eyes were not deceived by the hawk's apparent ease. Suddenly, like a flash of lightning, he hurtled down to the ground and with his sharp claws pierced his prey. It was not more than a few seconds before the hawk, wild and free, disappeared over a clump of trees. The Indians stared at the disappearing hawk in silence. After a while they resumed their walk.

They chattered gaily, and from time to time a sly remark would draw explosive laughter. Soon they had crossed the brown fields, climbed over a ditch and reached the highway. A truck passed them by and disappeared in a cloud of dust. The Indians walked past the first few scattered houses on the outskirts of the town. Faces appeared in the windows and watched the Indians as they walked towards the town. Imperceptibly the Indians moved closer together and hastened their steps.

They walked in silence until they reached the grocer's store. From the pockets of their shabby denims they collected a fistful of coins which they gave to True Blood, who entered the shop. The Indians propped themselves against the brick wall of the building and stared ahead expressionless. They pretended not to notice the policeman, swaggering back and forth, looking them up and down from the other side of the street.

The lady teacher appeared, her progress marked by the noise of her high-heeled shoes. For a fraction of a second, at the sight of Whispering Dawn, the steady beat of her walk faltered. Some vague sense of recognition stirred her conscience, but soon it was gone and the mechanical clickety-clack of her steps receded into the distance.

Meanwhile, in the store, True Blood waited his turn. People came in and went out carrying their purchases and the Indian, apparently oblivious of the passing time, stared at some cheap trinkets in a glass case. Eventually the store was empty and he was noticed by the grocer, who took the fistful of nickels and dimes and gave the Indian his tobacco.

When True Blood reappeared the Indians detached themselves from the wall and, followed by the suspicious stare of the policeman, disappeared down the road.

Notes on Sources

The Sweat Lodge. Sweat Lodge ceremonies exist to this day among the Ojibwa. "The Sweat Lodge" is based on ceremonies observed in 1955 on the shores of Red Lake in northwestern Ontario.

Blue Sky Takes a Wife. Collected 1955; Ojibwa; Lake Nipigon, northwestern Ontario. Parts of this story are closely related to the Winnebago Trickster cycle, in which the Trickster carries his sex organ in a box strapped to his back.

Nanabajou and His Daughter. Collected 1955; Ojibwa; Lake Nipigon, northwestern Ontario. Another story derived from the cycle of the Trickster. He unites in himself some of the traits of a god, an animal and a human being. He is a grotesque individual whose main physical features are enormous digestive and sexual organs.

The Evil Indian and the Orphan Girl. Collected 1956; Ojibwa; Snake Island, Lake Simcoe, southern Ontario. The basic character of the Evil Indian Man is that of a Trickster, who dupes others but who always comes to a bad end himself. He is cruel and possessed of a voracious sexual appetite which he is never allowed to satisfy.

The Bear Walker. Collected 1969; Mohawk; southern Quebec. Very similar to the Naskapi version in which the wife cohabits with a worm. The worm is killed by the husband who feeds it to her. She subsequently changes to a worm. In an Ojibwa version, the woman cohabits with a snake.

Big One and the Bad Medicine Woman. Collected 1971; Naskapi; Goose Bay, Labrador.

The Medicine Dream. Collected 1966; Ojibwa; Lake Nipigon, northwestern Ontario.

The Magic Gun. Collected 1955; Ojibwa; southern Saskatchewan.

Big Horn Gives Birth to a Calf. Collected 1969; Mohawk; southern Quebec.

The Preacher. Personal narrative of the "gentle Indian girl" to the author, 1955; western Ontario.

The Lady Teacher. Unpublished diary and personal narrative of the "lady teacher" to the author, 1969; Northwest Territories.

The Evil Spell. Personal narrative of "Rosana" to the author, 1955; northwestern Ontario.

The Indian and the Tall Fair Lady. Collected 1968; southeastern Quebec.

The Squaw Man. Collected 1955; northwestern Ontario.

Bibliographical Sources

James H. Chambers:
Journal of James H. Chambers - Fort Sarpy. p. 114, 158.

Rudolph F. Kurz:
Journal of Rudolph F. Kurz. Trans. Myrtis Jarrell, Bureau of American Ethnology. Bulletin CXV (1937) 176-177.

George Simpson:
George Simpson à Andrew Colville- 20 mai 1822; in F. Merk (éd.)
Fur Trade and Empire
George Simpson Journal (Cambridge, Mass.) pp. 182-3.

Matthew Cocking:
Ross's Fur Hunters of the Far West, p. 87.
E.E. Rich (ed.) Cumberland House Journals and Inland Journal 1775-1782. First Series 1775-1779 (London 1951) p. 47, 67.

James Isham:
Isham's Observations. p. 81.
Douglas MacTavish à Letitia MacTavish, 17 sept. 1834 in "The Hargrave Correspondence" 1821-43 (Toronto, Ont. 1938) pp. 153-4.

Pierre-Antoine Tabeau:
Taveau's Narrative: Five Indian Tribes of The Upper Missouri. p. 180.

David Thompson:
David Thompson's Narrative. pp. 234-5
Duncan Cameron "The Nipigon Country" 1804 and extracts of his journal.

David Lavender:
Bent's Fort. pp. 159-60.
The Fur Traders. Collections Chouteau (Ms in The Missouri Historical Soc., St-Louis, Missouri).

Duncan M'Gillivray:
The Nipigon Country, p. 248 ed. Morton, Journal of M'Gillivray, pp.60-1.

Alexander Henry:
New Light on the Early History of the Greater Northwest (ed. Elliott Coues)
The Manuscript Journals of Alexander Henry and of David Thompson (N.Y. 1897), 11:452.